W9-BFX-884

Critical Guides to French Texts

2 Camus: L'Etranger *and* La Chute

Critical Guides to French Texts

EDITED BY ROGER LITTLE, WOLFGANG VAN EMDEN,
DAVID WILLIAMS

CAMUS

L'Etranger *and* La Chute

Rosemarie Jones

Lecturer in French,
University of Sussex

Grant & Cutler Ltd

I.S.B.N. 84-499-4134-2

DEPÓSITO LEGAL: V. 2.279-1980

Printed in Spain by

Artes Gráficas Soler, S. A. - Olivereta, 28 - Valencia (18)

for

GRANT AND CUTLER LTD
11 BUCKINGHAM STREET, LONDON, W.C.2.

Contents

Prefatory Note

THE editions of *L'Etranger* and *La Chute* referred to in this study are the Folio paperback editions. Full details of these and of the standard editions of Camus's works are listed in the select bibliography. The following abbreviations have been employed in the body of the text:

> *Cah 1*: *Cahiers Albert Camus 1*
> *Cah 2*: *Cahiers Albert Camus 2*
> *P1*: Albert Camus, *Théâtre, récits, nouvelles* (Bibliothèque de la Pléiade)
> *P2*: Albert Camus, *Essais* (Bibliothèque de la Pléiade)

The figures in parentheses in italic type refer to numbered items in the select bibliography; the italic figure is usually followed by a page reference. Given the amount of critical writing devoted to Camus, the shortness of the bibliography represents a subjective and severely limited choice, but I have tried to include works which indicate a variety of approaches to Camus and which also suggest further reading. It has not been possible, for reasons of space, to acknowledge indebtedness to other critical suggestions apart from those of the authors listed in the bibliography. I should, however, like to express my warm thanks to Professor John Cruickshank for his constructive reading of the manuscript, and to Professor Roger Little as Advisory Editor.

Introduction

SINCE any text is based on certain assumptions, it is appropriate to begin by declaring those which, to the writer at least, appear most obvious. In the case of the present study, they are threefold.

Firstly, I have assumed that the title of the work is a useful working point from which to start and in addition, perhaps, a meaningful guide to interpretation. The care with which Camus chose his titles corroborates this assumption to some degree, and a list of the titles of the fictional works and essays alone is sufficient to reveal affinities between them: *L'Envers et l'endroit, Noces, L'Etranger, Le Mythe de Sisyphe, La Peste, L'Eté, L'Homme révolté, L'Exil et le royaume, La Chute*. Consistently, the titles illustrate the dominant image in the works and take a stand on the universal plane, claiming to speak generally and offering themselves for interpretation on the level of the human condition.

This, in part, is the justification for the approach adopted. Both *L'Etranger* and *La Chute* have been analysed many times and in a variety of different ways. If there is an emphasis in this study, it is on the protagonists not as characters in the sense of fully-rounded human beings with whom one might identify affectively, or into the recesses of whose minds one is privileged to peer, but as images of the way in which man tries to come to terms with his experience of himself and of the world in which he lives.

Thirdly, because Camus clearly invites the reader to extract a generalized significance from his works, and since he so consistently, and so successfully, abandons the narrative to the protagonist, I have tried to give a reading of the works as they offer themselves to the reader, as coming from Meursault and Clamence. This approach makes a certain

distinction necessary. The situations of Meursault and Clamence are part of general human experience, having common
validity: one can measure their experience against one's own.
However they remain created characters, and analysis of their
psychology is precisely that: examination of the psychology of
a literary creation, not the psychoanalysis of a living person.
As protagonists, they convince by their artificial approximation
to reality.

Fourthly, but more as a *caveat* than as an assumption, I
have not attempted to treat the intricate and space-consuming
problems of influences and composition.

1

L'Etranger: *Context*

'Dans deux ans écrire *une œuvre*'.
Camus, *Carnets*, April 1938

CAMUS'S first published novel was greeted with almost universal acclaim. *L'Etranger* seemed a title particularly appropriate to describe the nature and circumstances of the book itself just as much as its stated theme. The author was unknown to the French public and the novel seemed an enigma: both sober and disconcerting, presenting a reality so vivid as to appear hallucinatory, conveying the experience of French North Africa in terms of the French classical tradition.

Camus has subsequently become one of the most widely-known of French writers of this century, but the novel retains its mystery. It is not the aim of this study to dispel the mystery, but rather to reflect upon the theme of strangeness in the hope of coming closer to understanding what the novel says to us as readers. It is the text itself which speaks most clearly, but before examining the textual implications and development of the title image it is worthwhile to pause to consider the interface between *L'Etranger* and Camus's previous and contemporaneous writings. What types of preoccupation relate his early works among themselves? May consideration of Camus's other writings of the period enrich our understanding and appreciation of *L'Etranger*?

Some of Camus's earliest work remained unpublished or was available only in journals of the period. A representative selection has been collected in the *Cahiers Albert Camus 2*. These essays, written between 1932 and 1934, range from literary criticism: 'Un Nouveau Verlaine', 'Jehan Rictus', to a

poem 'Méditerranée' and imaginative essays: 'La Maison mauresque', 'Le Livre de Mélusine'.

Although these essays are miscellaneous, they are united
in the personal tone that pervades them and by a sense of
searching, epitomized in the quotation from Pascal with which
Camus prefaced 'L'Art dans la communion': 'Et je ne puis
approuver que ceux qui cherchent en gémissant'. It is the search
for form of a debutant writer, sometimes giving way to an
innate lyricism, at others consciously attempting to distil
emotion in detachment. It is also a search, if not for an
answer, then at least for a way of living with life's contradictions. For these are already clearly apparent to Camus: some
of the essays: 'Devant la morte', 'Perte de l'être aimé', 'L'Hô-
pital du quartier pauvre', form a meditation around death; in
contrast, 'Méditerranée' and 'La Maison mauresque' in particular, celebrate joy in being alive in a world of sun and
sensation. Camus seems to be pulled in two conflicting
directions. Much more clearly in these essays than at any time
in his subsequent work there comes across a quasi-mystical
search for some absolute transcending life itself: this leads
him to see in art 'un moyen d'arriver au divin' (*Cah 2*, 251),
and it is precisely the intuitive, emotive channels he associates
with art that Camus finds more reliable, more satisfying, than
intellectual reasoning; compared with intuition, 'l'intelligence
que nous considérons généralement comme claire et méthodi-
que n'est qu'un obscur et tortueux labyrinthe' (*Cah 2*, 193).
Yet against this, the Camus of these essays is already steeped
in the French intellectual tradition upon which he draws to
create them, and if all the arts proceed from 'une même
aspiration de l'esprit humain vers un monde meilleur d'oubli
et de rêve' (*Cah 2*, 172), Camus aspires also to depict that
world of the little people of Algiers with their suffering, their
illusions and their humour to which he also feels so close, and
so compassionate. Conscious of life's dualities, his truth lies in
acceptance of what life offers: 'Pas la révolte ni le désespoir.
La vie avec ce qu'elle a' (*Cah 2*, 239).

Camus's first published work was a short collection of
essays entitled *L'Envers et l'endroit*. These are based very

largely on personal experience and illustrate, more formally
and explicitly than the earlier essays, the contradictions of
experience suggested in the title: urban poverty and the wealth
of the natural elements, age and youth, death and life. The
narrator's attitude is a quasi-stoical awareness of the necessity
of accepting these vicissitudes: illness and death are inevitable,
but there is no need to anticipate them; life is to be lived in
the present. Two stories in 'L'Ironie' illustrate this point and
throw a revealing light on Meursault's behaviour after his
mother's death. The narrator recounts the story of an old
woman left at home while a group of young people go to the
cinema, and that of a lonely old man who tries unsuccessfully
to interest a group of young men in his stories of former days.
The destinies of the old people may be tragic, and the narrator
is fully conscious of their pathos, but 'qu'importent les souf-
frances d'un vieil homme quand la vie vous occupe tout entier?'
(*P2*, 18). The theme of duality and contradiction is carried
throughout the work. 'La Mort dans l'âme' relates both the
narrator's loneliness and disorientation in Prague and his joy
at returning via Italy and rediscovering the beauty of the
Mediterranean; in 'Amour de vivre' he responds to the evocations of both a cabaret turn in a Majorcan cafe and a gothic
cloister.

While the narrator in *L'Envers et l'endroit* invites, if not
a philosophical meditation, at least a reflection upon themes
of universal significance, the collection of essays entitled *Noces*
shows a resolute turning-away from problems posed by the
intellect: 'Hors du soleil, des baisers et des parfums sauvages,
tout nous paraît futile' (*P2*, 56). The essays celebrate the
theme of physical union, a sense of being a part of the natural
world through the body, catalysed by the luxuriant Algerian
nature and climate: 'Il me faut être nu et puis plonger dans
la mer, encore tout parfumé des essences de la terre, laver
celles-ci dans celle-là, et nouer sur ma peau l'étreinte pour
laquelle soupirent lèvres à lèvres depuis si longtemps la terre
et la mer' (*P2*, 57). The style of these essays is predominantly
lyrical, most appropriate perhaps to convey the intensely

subjective reactions of the narrator/experiencer, invaded by his sensations. Yet at the same time the narrator conveys a sense of the fundamental gap which separates man from nature: 'Il n'y a rien ici pour qui voudrait apprendre, s'éduquer ou devenir meilleur. Ce pays est sans leçons. Il ne promet ni ne fait entrevoir' (*P2, 67*). Since the natural context remains alien to man, offering nothing to the intellect and resisting any attempts on man's part to appropriate it, it follows that one must in all lucidity accept that the natural world can only be responded to in physical terms. The narrator of *Noces* endorses his instinctual response at a conscious level.

In this he is different from the young French Algerian men and women whom he observes on the beach and in the water with a sense of envy and of nostalgia. This 'race' epitomizes another kind of union: the human being perfectly in accord with his circumstances. They accept that life is over at thirty; until then, they drain the cup of the present. Unencumbered by intellectual imaginings, their response to life is direct and spontaneous. 'Mon camarade Vincent, qui est tonnelier et champion de brasse junior, a une vue des choses encore plus claire. Il boit quand il a soif, s'il désire une femme cherche à coucher avec, et l'épouserait s'il l'aimait ... Ensuite, il dit toujours: "Ça va mieux" — ce qui résume avec vigueur l'apologie qu'on pourrait faire de la satiété' (*P2, 69*). Although recognizing no allegiance to a wider framework of values, they nevertheless adhere to a simple pragmatic code. 'On a sa morale, et bien particulière. On ne "manque" pas à sa mère. On fait respecter sa femme dans les rues. On a des égards pour la femme enceinte. On ne tombe pas à deux sur un adversaire, parce que "ça fait vilain" ' (*P2, 72*). Meursault undoubtedly bears a close resemblance to the Vincent of *Noces,* as one of Camus's comments on *L'Etranger* would seem to indicate: 'ce que je vois surtout dans mon roman, c'est la présence physique, l'expérience charnelle que les critiques n'ont pas vue: une terre, un ciel, un homme façonné par cette terre et ce ciel. Naturellement, vous pouvez comprendre

Meursault, mais un Algérien entrera plus aisément et plus profondément dans sa compréhension'. [1]

These two collections of essays are revelatory in the light they shed on certain of the attitudes which Camus has attributed to Meursault, and in showing how his main themes in this period: the importance of the present, the contrasts of experience, are intimately connected with his experiences of Algeria. One should nevertheless beware of extrapolating from other sources on to *L'Etranger*. The dangers of this approach are illustrated in the way in which *La Mort heureuse,* Camus's first novel unpublished during his lifetime, has sometimes been taken to be a first draft of *L'Etranger*. It is the story of the search for happiness of Patrice Mersault. The search begins with a conscious decision to kill a man for his money. Not that Mersault kills from desire for gain; he kills in order to have freedom to concentrate on living and experiencing. As the novel proceeds, both the nature of the happiness Mersault is seeking and the way in which it can be achieved gradually become clear to him. He realizes that for him happiness lies not in travel, northern cities or even culture and civilization, nor in the constant company of other human beings, however tempting to palliate his solitude. Rather, it is alone, living on the Algerian coast, in close touch with the natural world, that he attains happiness, and that only after he has abandoned himself and learnt to live in tune with nature: 'le tout était de savoir s'humilier, d'ordonner son cœur au rythme des journées au lieu de plier le leur à la courbe de notre espoir' (*Cah 1,* 169). Mersault's conception of happiness is unusual, and might best be defined in three stages. Happiness is a state, not an emotion; as such, it can consciously be chosen. Consciously is the key word, for happiness is being aware of one's experiences and of one's life itself. This sounds simple, but the difficulty, the object of Mersault's quest, lies in cutting out what is accessory and concentrating on what is fundamental to oneself. This is what Mersault achieves: 'il rejoignait ainsi

---

[1] In an interview with Gaëtan Picon, *Le Littéraire,* 10 August 1946.

une vie à l'état pur, il retrouvait un paradis qui n'est donné qu'aux animaux les plus privés ou les plus doués d'intelligence. A ce point où l'esprit nie l'esprit, il touchait sa vérité et avec elle sa gloire et son amour extrêmes' (*Cah 1,* 171). Mersault dies shortly afterwards, but he accepts death as the inevitable *envers* of a life fully experienced, and he dies consciously, as he had lived; in these two cardinal senses it is, indeed, a happy death.

It is clear that the novel is similar in theme and orientation to *L'Etranger,* and considerable detail which Camus originally lent to Mersault was transmitted to Meursault. But it is not necessarily a reformulation of the same premisses: Meursault takes questioning further than his elder, and hesitates to be too explicit; the novel is the richer in force and ambiguity. Moreover *L'Etranger* is a much more subtly and limpidly structured novel; *La Mort heureuse* remains, to a degree, a pot-pourri of themes and episodes joined loosely, lacking in the rigour demanded only by the development of the narrative. Critics are virtually unanimous in endorsing Camus's decision not to publish at the time.

Camus originally regarded *L'Etranger* as part of a trilogy of writings centered around the notion of 'the Absurd': a novel, *L'Etranger,* two plays, *Caligula* and *Le Malentendu* and an essay, *Le Mythe de Sisyphe.* [2] Space precludes consideration of all the relevant works, but a brief examination of *Le Mythe de Sisyphe* is indispensable particularly since a body of critical opinion, from Sartre onwards, has seen that essay as a commentary on the novel. [3] *Le Mythe de Sisyphe* does not claim to be a philosophical essay: 'les pages qui suivent traitent d'une sensibilité absurde qu'on peut trouver éparse dans le siècle' (*P2,* 97); this does not prevent Camus from examining what he calls the only really major philosophical problem:

---

[2] 'Le thème qui m'intéressait avant la guerre, je l'ai traité sous trois formes différentes: l'essai dans *Le Mythe de Sisyphe,* le roman dans *L'Etranger,* le théâtre avec *Le Malentendu* et *Caligula',* quoted in Roger Quilliot, *La Mer et les prisons* (7, p. 92).

[3] 'M. Camus, dans *Le Mythe de Sisyphe* paru quelques mois plus tard, nous a donné le commentaire exact de son œuvre' (*10,* p. 93).

suicide. One commits suicide basically because one decides that life is not worth living; what interests Camus is whether, if one decides that life is not worth living, one should therefore in all honesty, and all logic, terminate one's life. But on what grounds might one make such a decision? For Camus the crux of the matter is what he calls 'l'absurde'. This is a two-term equation: on the one side is 'the world', by which is meant all experience outside man's mind; this is irreducible to reason and explanation. On the other side is man's tendency to seek for explanation, unity and meaning. 'The Absurd' is not a thing in itself: it is the confrontation between man's desire for clarity and the opacity of the world: 'ce qui est absurde, c'est la confrontation de cet irrationnel et de ce désir éperdu de clarté dont l'appel résonne au plus profond de l'homme' (*P2*, 113). As John Cruickshank has put it: 'the absurd is the conclusion arrived at by those who had assumed the possibility of a total explanation of existence by the mind but who discover instead an unbridgeable gulf between rationality and experience' (*2*, p. 49). It is in fact a debate between the absolute and the relative. Camus is quite prepared to concede that reason has its place: 'il est vain de nier absolument la raison. Elle a son ordre dans lequel elle est efficace' (*P2*, 124). The trouble is that, for Camus at least, man's desires are absolute: 'je veux que tout me soit expliqué ou rien' (*P2*, 117). And in founding 'the Absurd' Camus is coming down on the side of this absolute desire which finds a corresponding absolute refusal on the part of the world to accommodate to it. So if, as Camus holds, this is a truth which one discovers, then intellectual honesty demands that one stay with this truth, unlike a number of existentialist thinkers whom he sees as having evaded the logical consequences.

From his first premises, Camus draws a threefold conclusion: *révolte, liberté* and *passion*. None of these is precisely what it might seem. By *révolte* Camus means the perpetual tension of the irreconcilable duality between man and the world. *Liberté* is perhaps closest in meaning to independence: since there is no ultimate, sense-giving meaning in the world, man must think and act independently, and this may entail even rejection of any ideology based on the notion of man's freedom. *Liberté* can have meaning only in individual terms. By *passion* is meant 'la passion d'épuiser tout ce qui est donné' (*P2,* 142); a celebration and embracing of what this world offers, which is all that we have. For if there is no absolute, no essential unity or meaning, then conclusions based on *a priori* judgements must be questioned. An ethic of 'the Absurd' is founded not on the notion of quality, which is meaningless from this standpoint, but on the notion of quantity.

Camus gives three examples of 'l'homme absurde': ways of life lived according to this ethic. Don Juan, lover of many women, incorporates the question: 'Pourquoi faudrait-il aimer rarement pour aimer beaucoup?' (*P2,* 152). The actor chooses to portray, through his body, successive and transient lives, demonstrating 'à quel point le paraître fait l'être' (*P2,* 159). Finally, 'le conquérant', the man of action, chooses to identify with history, not with eternity. In all three cases, permanent values are rejected in favour of decisions based on present, avowedly ephemeral, realities. A fourth example of a living-out of 'the Absurd', on which Camus writes at some length, is art. Camus sees the work of art as consciously gratuitous and the artist, more particularly the novelist, as one who renounces explanation, relying on '[le] message enseignant de l'apparence sensible' (*P2,* 178).

To return to Camus's opening question, his arguments and examples combine to illustrate that life has no higher, transcendent meaning, but that it does not therefore follow that life is not worth living; on the contrary, life will be the more precious, the better lived, if one recognizes that life itself is the only palpable certainty. The closing and definitive image is that of Sisyphus, who risked the gods' anger and everlasting punishment to live a few more years 'devant la courbe du golfe, la mer éclatante et les sourires de la terre' (*P2,* 195). Consigned to hell and condemned, in eternity, to roll a rock to the summit of a mountain only to see it fall down again and recommence his task, Sisyphus symbolizes the eternal unsatisfactoriness of the human condition. His situation is tragic because he knows it to be futile, but this same knowledge enables him to rise above it. The task may be performed in sorrow or in joy; when the stone rolls down again and Sisyphus follows it he enjoys the brief respite of reflection, and in the uphill effort he possesses his rock, his physical struggle. 'Il faut imaginer Sisyphe heureux' (*P2*, 198).

Now clearly Meursault is not just another example of 'l'homme absurde', any more than *L'Etranger* is a fictional transposition of the arguments of *Le Mythe de Sisyphe*. On the other hand Meursault does illustrate perhaps the central preoccupation of the essay: the emphasis on life lived without any transcendent meaning. His trajectory, as we shall examine, illuminates the necessity for granting a limited place to reason although reason can never give access to the unity and clarity man continues to desire. That can only be glimpsed through intuitive, corporeal knowledge which, in turn, cannot be translated into demonstrable certainty. Meursault embodies the paradox of 'the absurd' and his closing words and experiences express a tension between the concrete and the reflective which leaves him, like Sisyphus, happy.

In the same way as Meursault is an independent character, so *L'Etranger* is an autonomous work, not bound to repeat what Camus wrote elsewhere. But even this brief look at other work preceding the novel and contemporaneous with it indicates the nature of Camus's concerns: the overriding preoccupation with man's experience in its diversity, contrasts and uniqueness, the search for a way of living based on empirical truths, yet remaining open to new experience, suspicion of that which distorts or conceals the realities of human existence. Such are the common elements which relate to one another Camus's works of this period; to what extent and in what way *L'Etranger* shares in that relationship are questions to be addressed to the text of the novel.

2

L'Etranger: *Part 1*

> 'I've asked myself many times: is there in the
> world any despair that would overcome this
> frenzied and, perhaps, indecent thirst for life in
> me, and I've come to the conclusion that, perhaps,
> there isn't. But, of course, that holds true only
> till I'm thirty'.
>
> Dostoievsky, *The Brothers Karamazov*

ON reading the first part of *L'Etranger,* one might well
wonder why Meursault should be termed an outsider.
To refer to someone in this way is perhaps in the first place to
characterize his relationships with other people, but if one
observes Meursault's interaction with others, there is little
evidence of his appearing different from them. He enters into
forms of relationship with Marie and Raymond, entertains
friendly relations with people in his immediate circle: Salamano, Céleste, Emmanuel; people he meets for the first time,
such as the concierge at the old people's home or Masson,
respond to him openly. He has a number of casual acquain-
tances in his neighbourhood, to judge from their greetings to
him (39). What is more, Meursault shows a certain sensitivity
towards others and a measure of tolerance and tact in his
dealings with them, trying to reduce the concierge's embarrass-
ment over a tactless remark (16) or restraining Raymond's
hotheadedness when they meet the Arabs on the beach. On
the whole, Meursault's relationships with other people appear
to be marked by mutual acceptance and the ability, on
Meursault's part, to deal with human situations as they occur.

Two exceptions might make one feel that Meursault seems
strange to other people: Marie's start on realizing, after the
afternoon on the beach, that Meursault is in mourning, and

his employer's indication that he finds Meursault strange for his lack of ambition. And from Meursault's point of view, if one goes beyond observation of his behaviour to take into account his expressed reflections, one finds that he is occasionally aware of a sense of being apart: conscious of a need to justify himself to his employer for having taken two extra days off; feeling that he is being judged by the old people in the home. He himself, however, describes the *femme automate* in the restaurant as *bizarre,* and in spite of getting on well with Masson, is critically aware of his habit of saying 'et je dirai plus'. These instances are significant and related. Meursault experiences himself as different when an explicit or implicit judgement is passed on him. Judgement in itself implies adherence to a norm of value by reference to which the judgement is made, and the common denominator of the judgements actually or seemingly applied to Meursault is social convention: the expectation that one should cultivate ambition or behave appropriately at or following a funeral. On the other hand the type of behaviour which Meursault censures is behaviour which is automatic: Masson's obsessive phrase which has nothing to do with what he is actually saying, the *femme automate*'s mechanical ticking of almost all the radio programmes listed in the magazine. So Meursault neither appears an outsider nor experiences himself as such in the reality of his interaction with others: it is judgement and evaluation which introduce the sense of being apart, and different from the norm on which judgement is based.

To turn from the human context to the natural environment, it is clear that the natural world: the sun, sky, sea, wind, temperature, light and darkness, informs the whole book with its presence, to such an extent that it is quite appropriate to speak of Meursault's having a relationship to it, since he is so conscious of its presence and effect upon him. Two of the elements in particular, the sea and the sun, play a part as significant in Meursault's life as any of his human contacts. The sea offers him ecstasy of movement in swimming, a sense of union and harmony in experiencing contact with the water. His relationship with Marie is closely connected with the

pleasures of the beach and the sea, and his attraction to her
resides partly in their shared enjoyment of the water and her
incorporation of the elements, her body glistening with water,
salt in her hair.

The role of the sun is much more ambiguous. In general
the sun is beneficial in providing the clear skies which move
Meursault so deeply and creating the warmth which penetrates
his body. In isolation from the effects it creates, however, the
sun appears inimical, as comes across clearly from the two
points of crisis in the first part: the funeral and the murder.
As the sun mounts in the sky on the day of the funeral, the
discomfort of those present increases to such a degree that
Meursault finds that 'l'éclat du ciel était insoutenable' (29).
The combined effects of the sun, his fatigue and the smells
which assail him make Meursault unable to see or to think
clearly (29); the sun even makes the surrounding countryside
seem 'inhumain et déprimant' (27).

In the passage leading up to and describing the murder
(85-95) an explicit parallel is drawn with the day of the
funeral: 'C'était le même soleil que le jour où j'avais enterré
maman'; the sun is mentioned some twenty times and almost
without exception is associated with malevolence: 'le soleil
tombait presque d'aplomb sur le sable et son éclat sur la
mer était insoutenable'; 'le soleil était maintenant écrasant'.
The closer Meursault approaches to the spring, and to the
Arab, the more vehemently does the sun seem to attack him;
he moves forward to avoid the sun, the Arab's knife flashes
in the sunlight, Meursault feels the sun's cymbals clash on his
forehead. At this point the sea and the sky, which formerly
had brought only pleasure to Meursault, appear to be in league
with the sun: 'la mer a charrié un souffle épais et ardent. Il
m'a semblé que le ciel s'ouvrait sur toute son étendue pour
laisser pleuvoir du feu. Tout mon être s'est tendu et j'ai crispé
ma main sur le revolver'. Should one conclude that the natural
elements are fundamentally hostile to man, and form an alli-
ance to bring about his downfall?

This would be too simple. Certainly Meursault feels op-
pressed by hostile elements at the time of the funeral and of

the murder, but he also experiences harmony and intimacy with those same elements at other times. What he feels on the affective plane is purely contingent and indicates no corresponding, anthropomorphic 'attitude' towards him on the part of nature. Nature simply exists, whether one thinks of it as an accomplice or as an enemy. Two passages in particular illustrate this. At the funeral the *infirmière déléguée* says to Meursault: 'Si on va doucement, on risque une insolation. Mais si on va trop vite, on est en transpiration et dans l'église on attrape un chaud et froid' (30). This could be read in the sense of 'loser loses all', implying an essential hostility on nature's part. That is what one may feel. But the point is that blazing sun will necessarily affect man's physical being, which is his point of insertion into the natural world, regardless of what he feels, thinks or decides. When Raymond and Meursault walk along the beach a second time and encounter the Arabs again, Meursault relates: 'tout s'arrêtait ici entre la mer, le sable et le soleil, le double silence de la flûte et de l'eau. J'ai pensé à ce moment qu'on pouvait tirer ou ne pas tirer' (91). Meursault is intensely aware of the natural world, but aware at the same time of its indifference towards whatever he or Raymond might choose to do. Even the word 'indifference', although Meursault uses it at a later stage (186), conveys only approximately the otherness of nature and the sense that there can be no relationship whatsoever between the natural world and questions of value. If Meursault feels he has destroyed 'l'équilibre du jour' (95), it is because he has broken the silence of the beach; that he has done so by a murderous shot is quite irrelevant in this context. So, ultimately, is the question of whether Meursault is *étranger* to the natural world or not. He may experience unity or discord, but the term itself has no relevance here.

If one widens the range of enquiry and examines one's own attitude to Meursault, it would be rare for a reader not to find him disconcerting, at least on an initial reading. This reaction is provoked less by what Meursault does or thinks than by what he fails to do or to register. Some of the most notable examples are the lack of expression of grief for his

mother, his indifference both to Raymond's proposal of friendship and to Marie's suggestion of marriage and his remark that
he finds the word *aimer* meaningless (69). Meursault's apparent
lack of concern for what are usually considered to be fundamental human issues is paralleled only by his seeming disregard
for the trivial. He eats eggs straight from the pan to save the
trouble of getting a plate, and replies to Raymond's question
as to what he thought of his *histoire* with: 'j'ai répondu que
je n'en pensais rien mais que c'était intéressant' (53).

Closer examination of each of these examples reveals,
however, that the indifference is more studied than natural.
Meursault's sentiments towards his mother are certainly not
lacking. His first thought on arriving at Marengo was to see
her body; she is mentioned in each chapter of this first part. [4]
Meursault becomes more involved with Raymond and the
thought of marriage to Marie takes root in his mind. He is
perfectly capable of putting himself out physically when he
swims, or when he runs after a lorry, capable also of thinking
and feeling: 'je le trouvais très gentil avec moi et j'ai pensé
que c'était un bon moment' (63). If he appears indifferent in
the cases cited, it is the result of a conscious choice.

This becomes clearer if one looks at precisely where his
indifference comes into play. In contrast to the relationship
with the natural world and the unevaluating tolerance characteristic of Meursault's relationships in general, he is here
confronted with the question of expression of thought and feeling. In assuming indifference, Meursault is refusing various
operations which intervene between his experience and its expression. As regards his mother's death he is refusing certain
conventions which are called moral: principally the assumption
that one should be seen to experience grief at a parent's death,
and incidentally that such grief should be filtered and expressed
through certain channels. Meursault's eating habits conflict

---

[4] Pingaud, in a section entitled 'Œdipe à Alger' has a clear summary of some of the psychological interpretations which bring out the
importance of the mother and absent father (*16*, pp. 72-8); see also
B. T. Fitch's 'Lecture psychanalytique' (*14*, pp. 78-89).

with what is conventionally acceptable; he satisfies his hunger directly, without regard for form or formality. His indifference to friendship or marriage is a refusal of the abstract notions which obscure the concrete reality; in practice Meursault supports Raymond, which is after all the meaning of being a *copain;* and it is when Meursault actually sees himself and Marie together as a couple, in the company of Masson and his wife, that the idea of marriage takes on meaning. He finds no meaning in the abstract, general verb 'to love' which is inadequate to convey the complex nature of attraction and attachment to a particular person. Finally, in seemingly refusing to think about what happened to Raymond, Meursault is rejecting not all thought, but a type of speculative thought based on something outside his own experience. So Meursault's indifference is a rejection of abstraction, generalization, evaluation, speculation: all processes which, like convention, interpose a screen between what is experienced and what is expressed. Meursault prefers to live as far as possible without the screen. His strangeness to the reader stems partly from this rejection of precisely those processes of thought to which the reader is accustomed and upon which, as a reflective human being, he probably prides himself.

The attack, however, goes further to aim at the whole business of reading. For Meursault as narrator rejects the same processes he rejects as protagonist, insofar as they apply to the work of fiction. In devoting twice as much space to the loss of Salamano's dog as to the discussion of marriage with Marie, [5] Meursault refuses to comply with the reader's expectations of what is important in the novel. Meursault's refusal to anticipate events, with the single exception of the 'quatre coups brefs que je frappais sur la porte du malheur' (95), parallels his rejection of speculative thought. And when he does not say what he is thinking, or does not expand on his reactions to events, he revokes the reader's privilege of receiving an explanation from the narrator. It is perhaps this refusal on Meursault's — and Camus's — part to provide eluci-

---

[5] Respectively 64 and 32 lines, pp. 63-65 and 69-70.

dation which most estranges the reader. 'Tout comprendre c'est tout pardonner', but there is a certain high-handedness in Meursault's request, even demand, to be read and deciphered. [6] Although there may be a trace of Romantic haughtiness in the protagonist-narrator and his creator, there is perhaps a further reason for Meursault's turning-away from the reader. In spite of all the reader's efforts to comprehend him, Meursault retains opacity, separated from us both by his attitudes as protagonist and by the chosen form and manner of narration. Because Meursault remains opaque, the reader is given direct experience of his otherness and experiences himself in some degree as an outsider in the world of the novel he has entered.

The last movement in the quartet of relationships in the first part is to explore whether Meursault could be seen as a stranger to himself. In the same way as his relationship to others and to the natural world is characterized by an acceptance of things as they are, so Meursault accepts the sensations which experience offers him. He is totally involved in the sensation for itself quite irrespective of whether another might judge the context to be pleasant or sorrowful, trivial or important. Being at his mother's grave does not prevent him from being sensitive to the richness of the colours in the cemetery. Any experience is material for Meursault's attention, an attention which is active and aware, but which again cuts out anything beyond the present sensation which might distort that sensation or detract from it. As Sartre has noted, the consciousness of Meursault is 'transparente aux choses et opaque aux significations' (*18,* p. 107). Meursault welcomes his experience and responds to it in its own terms: sensations are isolated, successive and ephemeral, and that is how Meursault perceives and records them, celebrating the diversity, discontinuity, even the monotony of his experience. In this he achieves a singular harmony between his experience, his attitude and his expression which is happiness in all but name.

---

[6] For a critical view of provocation on the part of Meursault and Camus, see Leo Bersani's article 'The Stranger's Secrets' (*10*).

The first part of the book ends on the word *malheur* and the harmony is abruptly broken. It is significant that in the passage describing the murder, all the forms of relationship examined up to this point are present, developed and intensified. [7]

The other human being is the Arab. Meursault's previous relations with him were neutral: simple acceptance of his existence and of his grudge against Raymond. Now the otherness of this man comes into play and predominates over Meursault's usual tolerance. No words are spoken, Meursault's perception is distorted and he thinks the man is laughing. The fact that the man is an Arab accentuates the gap of language and communication. The man is shown in all his opacity. The light and heat of the sun become so bright, so strong, that the balance Meursault had previously enjoyed between the coolness of the water and the warmth of the sun has given way and the sun dominates everything, making the sea boiling metal, the sky a sheet of flame. Neither the Arab nor the sun have changed, but in Meursault's perception they have become so intensified that they are pure otherness, more themselves and therefore strange to Meursault. With this he cannot cope: the harmony upon which his way of living had been based is destroyed and in that instant Meursault is a stranger to himself. He pulls the trigger and for the first time at the time, evaluates his action, giving it an interpretation, becoming vulnerable and open to judgement: 'j'avais détruit l'équilibre du jour, le silence exceptionnel d'une plage où j'avais été heureux'.

Finally, Meursault tests to the limit any relationship the reader may have established with him. We may have been prepared to take Meursault seriously and try to understand him, but are we to accept a murder? It may not be too fanciful to suggest that in killing the Arab Meursault symbolically kills

---

[7] G. V. Banks analyzes certain other passages in the first part where, as in the scene of the murder, the same elements are present: Meursault, another human being, an effect upon the senses by the surrounding (predominantly natural) world, sleep and death (*8*, pp. 38-40).

the reader. His relation to the Arab, apart from restraining Raymond, had been restricted to his written involvement in composing Raymond's letter; the relationship with the reader depends solely upon the written word.

So the murder is committed. It is not yet a question of evaluating what has occurred: the reader is simply presented with the experience as it happened to Meursault. Judgement is the affair of the second part.

3

L'Etranger: *Part 2*

'it is not necessary to accept everything as true, one must only accept it as necessary'.

Kafka, *The Trial*

IN the second part a profound change marks Meursault's relationship with others. The people he encounters are no longer individuals but anonymous functionaries: *le juge d'instruction, le procureur, l'aumônier*. When the individuals of his previous life appear, they have become witnesses for the defence, and communication with them is only possible through the lawyers. In the second part, then, Meursault encounters society, the collective institution of human beings. Naturally society had existed before, but Meursault had been able to avoid dealing on the institutional level in his chosen attitude and, for example, in his dislike and avoidance of the police (62). Now, however, society claims him and avoidance is no longer possible.

The largest section of the second part is concerned with Meursault's trial: he comes up against one of the most formalized aspects of society — its legal system. Now a trial, including the preliminary enquiry or *instruction* characteristic of French law, is an enquiry into the circumstances surrounding the commission of a crime, in order to be able to pass the sentence thought appropriate. That is to say that a trial is concerned largely with questions of motive: this is all the difference between murder and homicide. If one looks for the motive for the murder, it is there in the text, clear to Meursault and to the reader. As W. M. Frohock has shown in a study of the metaphors in the murder passage: 'Camus' metaphors are simultaneously the vehicle of the drama and the

instrument of psychological analysis. For by following the
play of metaphor we also follow the play of hallucination in
Meursault's mind, and among the hallucinations is hidden
— for all to see! — the motive for the otherwise inexplicable
murder of the Arab . . . he shoots — because he has had the
hallucination of being attacked by the actual weapon which
has already harmed his friend Raymond. Nothing could be
simpler nor, given the confused state of Meursault's mind,
more comprehensible: he shoots in self-defense.' (*15*, pp. 95-6).

The 'motive' Meursault proffers: 'c'était à cause du soleil'
(158) does not satisfy the court, for what he gives is a description. What the judges want, and what we as readers want
if we still find the murder problematical, is an explanation.
And description and explanation are processes of a quite different order.

We shall return to this point, but it is necessary first to
look at the way in which the trial is carried out. Now certain
aspects of the trial are patently not credible. One would
certainly expect the defence to call Meursault's employer as
witness, by virtue of his social standing; one would assume,
likewise, that a plea of self-defence would be made; finally,
it is most improbable that in the Algeria of the time, a prov-
ince of France, a French Algerian would be condemned to
death for the murder of an Arab. To present the trial in this
way is clearly the choice of the author, not the protagonist:
Meursault can only record what happens to him, not manip-
ulate his circumstances. Camus however does not hesitate to
alter the probable circumstances in order to secure Meursault's
execution.

The trial, obviously, is presented from Meursault's viewpoint. But while in the first part his recording of experience
was relatively neutral, here he is presenting a satirical picture
of the proceedings. This sets the tone of the account of the
spirit in which the trial is carried out. 'Justice' depends upon
the adroitness with which arguments are presented, and the
participants clearly regard the trial as a contest of skill. The
prosecution establishes a necessary connection with the par-
ricide which simply happens to come up for trial next; the

papers magnify the issue to create more sensation in the summer lull. The robes, the procedures, the self-important comings and goings, all combine to produce the impression of theatricality and, as Robert Champigny has shown, the account of the trial represents an indictment of 'la société théâtrale' (*12,* p. 34).

But the theatricality, and the comedy which accompanies it, mask something more sinister. Under the pretext of trying to understand Meursault's action, those concerned with the trial are in fact doing something very different. They are trying to 'understand' not in his terms but in theirs, which amounts to finding meaning in what Meursault did. What they cannot understand is that he committed a murder apparently without motive. It is already indicative that for them there can be no understanding without motive, but the process is taken further and, since no meaning can be found in the act itself, meaning is imposed upon it from without, and this by a threefold method.

In the first place it is assumed that there must be something, a species of first cause, behind the act. Enquiry is therefore directed backwards to Meursault's previous brush with organized society, his mother's funeral, and a necessary causal link is established between the two events. Secondly, a chain of reasoning is constructed, which runs something like this. Meursault has committed a crime. This makes him a criminal, and a criminal is a moral monster (147). Show this, and his crime becomes understandable. The spurious logic betrays its dependence upon a dubious rationalism and upon the third element in the process — the imposition of value judgements and the assumptions they in turn rely upon. The result of all this — an explanation which, as Meursault recognizes, is plausible — bears no relation to what actually happened.

As we have noted, Meursault's viewpoint is a satirical one, and this implies both a condemnation of an existing state of affairs and a vision of another order of things which contrasts with the one under review. The basis on which the trial proceeds forms a diametrical contrast with Meursault's attitude as it emerges from the first part. Society works on the belief that an explanation can be given for an occurrence. The explanation, in turn, is based on assumptions of causality and rational argument. The data are abstracted and generalized and emphasis placed on the coherence and logic of the argument. By contrast, Meursault refuses to recognize causal links, abstraction and precisely the type of reasoning for reasoning's sake upon which the arguments of the trial depend. His focus is the event itself in all its fragmentation and disorder, without explanation and without evaluation. In order however to appreciate more fully the implications of Meursault's refusal, it is necessary to look more explicitly at what he is confronting.

For it is not purely the legal system which makes him a martyr to his beliefs. The legal system acts in the book simply as a paradigm — albeit a most forceful and appropriate one — of the mechanisms by which society operates. Indeed the legal system is only the judicial arm of society: in itself it is impotent and theatrical, receiving its force only through the belief and assent of society; Meursault is condemned not in the name of the law but 'au nom du peuple français' (164). It is only because convention asserts that a man should show grief at his mother's funeral that Meursault's conviction can be secured. As Camus noted: 'Dans notre société tout homme qui ne pleure pas à l'enterrement de sa mère risque d'être condamné à mort' (*11,* p. 1). After the trial, Meursault's rejection of the viewpoint of the chaplain goes beyond societal convention to include also those values upon which society claims to be based, the Judaeo-Christian ethic. Indeed, it is not merely the chaplain who represents these values: he is, if anything, their most sympathetic advocate in the novel. The *juge d'instruction* admits that his life is given meaning by his faith (108), and implicit in the trial are the commandments: 'Thou shalt not kill', and 'Honour thy father and thy mother, that thy days may be long in the land which the Lord thy God giveth thee'.

Meursault's attitude, then, represents a radical questioning not only of the legal system but also of the society which empowers it and of the values which inform that society. It would however be premature to assume that Meursault's con-

demnation of society in the second part is a function simply
of his attitude as expressed in the first part: in other words, it
remains an open question whether Meursault becomes a stranger to himself in the course of part two.

In killing another human being, Meursault has made
himself an outsider from society, from the company of good
and reasonable men of which society likes to think it is
composed. That however is the sum total of his communication
with society, which takes up his gesture and carries it further.
The murder, in Meursault's terms, might be interpreted as a
refusal to remain within society, but society refuses to tolerate
rejection. Meursault is a threat, so society does its utmost to
anodize his gesture. While it appears to set him apart, in
labelling him a criminal, society is in fact attempting to draw
him under its net. This goes from inserting him into society
from the point of arrest, to eventual disposal via execution.
For if Meursault can be brought to accept the image of
himself which society offers, reply to the questions which
it poses, assent to the explanations it presents, then he has
been made 'étranger à lui-même' and society has triumphed.
So even before the trial proper, the *juge d'instruction* insists
that Meursault play the game by explaining himself (106); he
is supplied with a lawyer whether or not he requests one
(99-100); his private experience is exposed to public scrutiny
during the trial and expressed in society's terms: 'J'ai mis du
temps à le comprendre [le procureur], à ce moment, parce
qu'il disait "sa maîtresse" et pour moi, elle était Marie' (153).
Although nominally the centre of his trial, Meursault is in fact
reduced to nothing (159).

During the *instruction* and trial Meursault appears to be
reacting in very much the same way as he did before his imprisonment, refusing any interpretation and re-stating his experience as he had lived it: 'c'était à cause du soleil', saying
precisely what he thinks regardless of how it may appear
to the judgement of others: 'Sans doute, j'aimais bien maman,
mais cela ne voulait rien dire. Tous les êtres sains avaient plus
ou moins souhaité la mort de ceux qu'ils aimaient' (102). His
reactions provoke the discomfort, exasperation or laughter of

the members of 'la société théâtrale', and Meursault's demonstration of this theatricality draws part of its force from the fact that his own attitude is contrasting. His persistence in being himself, in opposition to the hypocrisy of society, makes him in this respect a martyr to truth, as Camus described him: 'On ne se tromperait ... pas beaucoup en lisant dans *L'Etranger* l'histoire d'un homme qui, sans aucune attitude héroïque, accepte de mourir pour la vérité' (*11,* p. 2).

Meursault's appearances before the *juge d'instruction* and at the trial constitute the 'external' element of the second part. At the risk of oversimplification, one could say broadly that this is paralleled by an 'internal' element: the time Meursault spends in his cells.

During his imprisonment Meursault goes through four rather different stages of experience. The first comprises the first few days in prison: from the 'external' point of view, Meursault shares a cell with other prisoners, mainly Arabs (113-4), the first formal interrogations take place (99) and after being isolated in a cell of his own, he receives a visit from Marie (114-9). At this point he does not really feel that he is in prison. His thoughts are 'des pensées d'homme libre' (119); he expects events to occur (113) and still has desires for women, cigarettes, swimming. He continues to have such thoughts for some months. So this overlaps with what Meursault clearly marks out as the start of a different period: 'C'est seulement après la première et la seule visite de Marie que tout a commencé' (113); 'C'est peu après qu'elle m'a écrit. Et c'est à partir de ce moment qu'ont commencé les choses dont je n'ai jamais aimé parler' (119). This second stage, which is described in the second chapter of part two, parallels the *instruction* in which Meursault is invited to reflect on what *had* happened; in his cell he is concerned with the absence of women and of cigarettes, he sleeps, which is a lack of activity, and he reflects on the story of the Czech, an event which happened, but not to him. Finally, he discovers memory. While memory is for Meursault primarily a remembrance of things physical, of the furniture in his flat, it is nevertheless a mental activity. So during this period of five months Meursault, cut off from the sensory experiences associated with his former life, lives from their absence, lacking and distant, prolonging mentally the physical sensation.

When he is again seen in his cell after the trial and sentence, a further change has taken place, which the fifth chapter illuminates. Meursault's concern now is with the alternative possibilities of his appeal and his execution: in other words the matter of his reflection is now purely the possibilities which society has presented to him: his past life has dropped away. This in a sense is only natural, given his condition; what is more significant is the manner of his reflection. He is in fact imagining, speculating, reasoning: precisely those activities which he had previously rejected. Meursault has interiorized those processes which had been employed at the trial. But this leaves him in a twofold dilemma. On the one hand, the adopted processes of reasoning are unable to master the fundamental, instinctive desire to go on living: 'ce qui me gênait un peu dans mon raisonnement, c'était ce bond terrible que je sentais en moi à la pensée de vingt ans de vie à venir' (173). And the stubborn beat of his heart, the rhythm of his corporeal existence, conflicts with the workings of his imagination: 'J'essayais ... de me représenter une certaine seconde où le battement de ce cœur ne se prolongerait plus dans ma tête. Mais en vain' (171). Secondly, even when he does manage, through reason, to rationalize and subjugate his instinctive reactions, this produces no lasting satisfaction. The most he can hope to achieve is 'une heure de calme' (174): Meursault is still caught in the inescapable oscillation between pardon and execution; thought can only exacerbate the contradiction, cannot alter the situation.

Here Meursault touches his nadir. It is a powerful portrayal of the reflections of a condemned man, reduced to the vagaries of hope. But it is also the statement of a crisis of a different order. Meursault's story is that of a man who had lived happily on an instinctive, spontaneous level and who finds that he can no longer ignore the demands of the mind. His abrupt exclusion from Eden, through the murder, is followed by a gradual recession of the image of that paradise, and at the same time, a slow fall into consciousness of mentality. But the life of the mind, to which Meursault awakens, is no substitute paradise, but first a limbo and then a kind of hell, filled with questions which he cannot avoid, but cannot solve. Moreover the body continues to act instinctively, a living reminder of paradise lost. The problem is that if one lives in the body, instinctively, that can only be an ephemeral paradise: the mind will awaken. But if one tries to live only in the mind, one risks not only the possible distortion of a purely intellectual view, one is exposed also to the *hasard* of physical demands, which may undermine even the most rigorous system of thought. Meursault is body and mind, caught in a disjunction between living in the body and living in the mind, the one no longer possible, the other a perpetual discomfort.

The fourth stage in Meursault's inner life is marked by the visit of the prison chaplain and Meursault's outburst to him. As we have seen, the chaplain incarnates those values on which society is founded, on which Meursault's condemnation is based, and which Meursault rejects. But the chaplain also represents a culmination of a different cype, for he presents the Christian faith as going beyond human justice, as encompassing not only man's physical death but also the destiny of his immortal soul. Serene in his 'totalitarian' view, the chaplain represents an attitude composed of three elements, which he proffers for Meursault's assent: the rejection of immanence in favour of transcendence, the abdication of pride and independence in recognizing oneself as a sinner; the vehicle of prayer, which means that the solution of one's questions and contradictions is committed to God's infinite wisdom. Against this, Meursault in his outburst and afterwards refuses not only the privileged viewpoint of the Christian faith, in his rejection of any *a priori* values or interpretation; he reaffirms the immanence of his life, his right to live it as he wishes, and, in his hope that he will be greeted at his execution with 'des cris de haine' (186), he also accepts, even welcomes, the tensions and contradictions he lives and embodies. In reaffirming himself, his life and his identity, Meursault reattains

the harmony he had already lived, and for the first time qual-
ifies himself as *heureux* (186).

At the same time as Meursault in this movement becomes
reconciled to himself, he also opens himself for the first time
'à la tendre indifférence du monde' (186). In fact the natural
world had not ceased to accompany him through the second
part: he had remained sensitive to the heat in the courtroom,
to sensations intruding from outside, to the beauty of the
evening; in short, the natural elements, and the sounds of the
life of Algiers outside the courtroom walls, are indelibly associated with his previous life (148-9). Yet the natural world
again remains indifferent, as it had been at the time of the
murder. 'Comme si les chemins familiers tracés dans les ciels
d'été pouvaient mener aussi bien aux prisons qu'aux sommeils
innocents' (149). And if Meursault only rejoins the indifference of the world *for the first time* at the end of the book,
it is because it is only when one has become involved with
questions of meaning and value that one can be truly indifferent. In asserting the equivalence of all things, Meursault
endorses consciously the acceptance characteristic of his earlier
instinctive attitude.

This does, however, raise a problem. We know that Meursault had been a student, and his intimation is that when
he discontinued his studies he consciously put away ambition
(69). It seems unlikely that Meursault could have been a
student without becoming aware of the demands of the mind.
It would seem that the incongruity stems from the conflicting
elements which Camus wished to portray through his protagonist. Camus needed a man whose existence was based on
his concrete, physical experiences, in order to show Meursault's attitude to those experiences. He also needed Meursault's
attitude to be a conscious one in order that it should be shown
the more clearly and forcefully. Further, Camus needed Meursault to be sufficiently naïve for the trial to appear strange to
him, and sufficiently aware to be able to convey its strangeness.
Meursault has to appear both mindful and non-reflective,
conscious and spontaneous; he is perhaps charged with too
much for all these elements to be coherent with themselves.

Whether or not one regards this as a mark of the inexperienced novelist, it remains true that Meursault's own contradictions are consistent with the acceptance of discrepancy which he expresses.

So Meursault is reconciled to himself, and to the natural world. Does he still remain *étranger* to the reader? In one important sense he is closer to the reader in the second part than in the first; as here his mental life predominates, with all that implies of reflection and comment, this brings him closer both to what the reader expects from fiction and to the reader's own habits. However there is, as one might expect, a corresponding movement away. By the time the reader has read the account of the trial, he has probably rejected the prosecution's view of Meursault and is working out his own interpretation, as indeed the book seems to invite him to do. But it is here that the problem arises, for how is the reader to make any interpretation? Meursault's attack is more than a simple attack on society, its instruments and conventions: it questions the relevance of any *a priori* values, the validity of any interpretative framework. Is it 'true' to say that Meursault is 'un brave homme' (145), or 'un honnête homme, un travailleur régulier, infatigable, fidèle à la maison qui l'employait, aimé de tous et compatissant aux misères d'autrui' (159), any more than it is to say that '[il] n'en avai[t] point d'âme, et que rien d'humain, et pas un des principes moraux qui gardent le cœur des hommes ne [lui] était accessible' (155)? Perhaps we have to renounce judgements of that kind, but what do we do then? It is here that the reader finds himself most radically alienated, for how can one do without judgement?

A case in point is provided by the question of whether Meursault is guilty or not guilty. This is the pivotal judgement in the trial, and one which the reader in turn feels called to make. In legal terms, Meursault is guilty. The prosecution and the jury find him guilty of murder; we may feel that a verdict of manslaughter would have been more appropriate, and the essential difference, as we have seen, highlights the attitudes and assumptions of society as they are presented in the novel. But if one respects the relevance of the terms

of guilty and innocent in the legal context, one cannot dis-
agree that Meursault is guilty of a crime. If, by contrast, we
feel, however obscurely, that Meursault is somehow innocent,
this can only be to the extent to which we have been brought
to question the hold of these concepts on reality. If one judges,
Meursault is guilty; the only way in which a notion of innocence or 'non-guilt' may be preserved is by abstaining from
judgement.

Ultimately, this will not be possible. But if we are brought
to suspend our judgement on Meursault during his trial, Meursault has made his case, and that in two ways. He will have
brought us to re-read the book, to re-examine the evidence
independently of the prosecution's case, which amounts effectively to the success of Meursault's appeal; secondly, he will
have led us for a time, the time of re-reading and thought, to
replace judgement with observation of experience, to substitute
for the static, staccato imposition of judgement the dialectical,
dynamic experience of observing and reflecting.

Finally, although we shall pass judgement upon Meursault
and leave *L'Etranger,* the process of narration itself provides
a triumphant vindication of Meursault's approach to experience.

There is a marked difference in the style and tone of
the two parts. Broadly, the first part is episodic, concrete
and deals in relatively short time-sequences which are fairly
clearly delimited by the use of *aujourd'hui, demain, hier,* and
the naming of the days of the week. By contrast the second
part is organized around the three stages of the *instruction,* the
trial and the period following; events are defined not by the
days on which they take place but by the order imposed upon
them: so much time occupied by the *instruction* and trial.
The first part looks like a form of journal, the second like
a *récit* in which the narrator organizes and evaluates his experience. Now in a sense one accepts without question the
poetic time of narration as reflecting Meursault's experience
of the moment. If he chooses to say 'Aujourd'hui, maman est
morte', or in the second part to recount his experiences in
periods of weeks and months rather than days, this does not

shake our confidence in Meursault as narrator nor in the credibility of the world of the novel.

Yet if one chooses to pursue the point and identify the different moments of narration, one discovers a pattern of overlapping time-sequences. When Meursault rediscovers memory, in what has been described as the second stage of his imprisonment, he returns in imagination for short periods of time to his previous surroundings: 'Je me mettais quelquefois à penser à ma chambre et, en imagination, je partais d'un coin pour y revenir en dénombrant mentalement tout ce qui se trouvait sur mon chemin' (122). In the same way, Meursault relives episodes in his former life, and the narration of the first part is a re-visitation of his past in shorter or longer periods, defined at first precisely with *aujourd'hui, demain, hier,* growing gradually less distinct as his grip on his previous way of living loosens. This takes place during the time of the *instruction,* as is indicated by the mention at the end of the second chapter of part two: 'Mais en même temps et pour la première fois depuis des mois, j'ai entendu distinctement le son de ma voix. Je l'ai reconnu pour celle qui résonnait déjà depuis de longs jours à mes oreilles et j'ai compris que pendant tout ce temps j'avais parlé seul' (126). In part compensation for his present inactivity, in part affirmation of his truth, Meursault's narration counterbalances the life he has been forced to lead. Similarly, the *instruction* and trial are narrated after they have taken place, the *instruction* after its completion and the trial after Meursault has been sentenced. Here the narration shows the hindsight afforded by distance and the extent to which Meursault has gradually internalized the processes employed by the legal arm of society, enabling him to describe from inside the society which has begun to take him over.

However at the beginning of the final chapter of the book Meursault once again employs the present of narration: 'Je n'ai rien à lui dire, je n'ai pas envie de parler, je le verrai bien assez tôt...' (165). I would suggest that the opening lines of the final chapter, up to 'couché, je passe les mains sous ma tête et j'attends', describe Meursault after the chaplain's visit recounted later. [8] Meursault has now reasserted his own truth, and he can now reinstate the present instead of having to speak in the past; he can begin in the present and move into the past because the past has now caught up with the present, has been assimilated through and following Meursault's outburst to the chaplain.

Each part of the book, then, presents Meursault's experience both as it seemed to him at the time and in the light of subsequent experience, which colours and orientates the presentation. The structure reflects the tension between living experience and reflecting on experience, living with what one knows and accommodating to what is strange, with which the book is concerned. Meursault's final experiences and the narration of the beginning and end of the last chapter express the equilibrium which is finally achieved between revolt and consent; the present inserted here into the past creates a sense of timelessness, and it is significant that the novel should end with its verbs in the subjunctive, as mood takes over from temporality.

---

[8] It is not, I think, contradictory that Meursault should say: 'Pour la troisième fois j'ai refusé de voir l'aumônier' (165) when in fact the chaplain had entered his cell (175). Meursault had still refused to see him (174): the chaplain had come in uninvited.

4

L'Etranger: *Form and Style*

> 'don't think that I've spoken so candidly about your faces now because I'm simple-minded. Oh no, not at all! Perhaps I, too, have something in mind'.
>
> Dostoievsky, *The Idiot*

ONE of the most salient features of *L'Etranger* is the author's concession of the narrative to the protagonist. Meursault, as protagonist and narrator, uses those fictional forms most appropriate to the rendering of his experience in both parts of the novel. In the first and second parts respectively, Meursault employs conventions associated with the *journal* and the *récit*. The journal form carries with it the convention of direct expression by the subjective consciousness. Of all the fictional forms available to the author/narrator, the journal perhaps conveys most nearly the flux of living; events are noted as they occur with no apparent prior disposition of material nor interpretation. The *récit* presupposes prior evaluation; its form permits the narrator, often the subject of the *récit,* to reexamine his past in the light of subsequent experience. [9] The last chapter of the novel displays an unusual merging of the journal and *récit* forms, most apt to convey the synthesis of approaches to experience which Meursault at that point illustrates.

The use of these forms entails two related considerations. Although one is scarcely conscious of Camus's presence as

---

[9] The *récit* is discussed again later in connexion with *La Chute*, pp. 75-76.

author, [10] he is nevertheless, obviously, responsible for the organization of the book which subsumes Meursault's narration. On the one hand Meursault gives his experiences in their isolation and fragmentation as he lived them, on the other Camus allows Meursault to recount only those experiences which have a bearing on the orientation of the novel as a whole. In this latter perspective, as Sartre has noted, 'le plus petit incident a du poids; il n'en est pas un qui ne contribue à conduire le héros vers le crime et vers l'exécution capitale' (*18*, p. 112). So the different episodes are both isolated and interconnected. This paradoxical structure must, I think, inevitably characterize any fictional work of this type, in which a narrator recounts in apparent independence from an author. In this novel, however, the emphasis on fragmentation relates not only to the manner of narration but also to the matter of what Meursault is conveying in the first part especially: a particular way of approaching experience. This sets up a double tension between the narration and the book, the narrator and the author, as Meursault tends towards chaos and Camus's effort must be towards integration; Meursault's orientation would lead to destruction of the book and Camus's imperative is to write it. From this tension springs some of the fundamental ambiguity of the book: Camus brings Meursault to the point of expressing his experience but Meursault's preference is not to explain himself: the result is a statement devoid of explanation.

Secondly, we have noted that Meursault in his expression endeavours to remain as close as possible to the sensation or experience itself. Now obviously this must be a relative matter: the whole narrative is filtered through Meursault's consciousness and we as readers are unable to apprehend his experience

---

[10] Camus acknowledged his own intervention in Meursault's scene with the chaplain: 'Avec l'aumônier, mon Etranger ne se justifie pas. Il se met en colère, c'est très différent. C'est moi alors qui explique, direz-vous? Oui, et j'ai beaucoup réfléchi à cela. Je m'y suis résolu parce que je voulais que mon personnage soit porté au seul grand problème par la voie du quotidien et du naturel. Il fallait marquer ce grand moment.' *Carnets* janvier 1942-mars 1951, 29-30.

in its brute state. Nevertheless some of the most striking stylistic features of the narration serve the purpose of rendering most immediately *le vécu* of Meursault. While the past historic, the conventional literary tense, tends to deal with actions now completed, definite, and to emphasize their place in a seriality of events, the perfect tense, which preponderates in *L'Etranger,* defines actions by reference to a present, still open and uncompleted, and emphasizes the uniqueness and independence of events. Moreover, the emphasis falls not so much on the chain of events, as it does with a succession of past historics, as on the place of the event in the continuing experience of the subject.

The use of the first person in the novel is consistent with the attempt to convey the experience of the subjective consciousness. The *je* conventionally entails a degree of authenticity: one assumes that the narrator has undergone the experiences he relates, and that events occurred approximately as they are recounted. Yet in other respects Meursault departs from first-person convention. It is traditional also for the first-person narrator to be omniscient in that which relates to his experience, and for there to be established between narrator and reader a bond of familiarity and complicity, since the reader enjoys the privilege of entering into the narrator's mind. Meursault continually frustrates the reader by refusing to conform to his expectations. What is important to him is the close rendering of his sensations and reactions; those of a hypothetical reader are of secondary importance. As many commentators have noted, Meursault's *je* approximates to an *il:* we know no more than if we were observing him from the outside. Camus acknowledged that he had utilized certain modern American fictional techniques in writing *L'Etranger,* and these have clearly been brought to bear on the narrative viewpoint, as also on the principal tone of the narration.

Broadly, one finds in *L'Etranger* three preponderant styles or tones. Perhaps the most striking is the much-commented neutral tone in which most of the first part is written, and which captures attention from the initial 'Aujourd'hui, maman est morte' (9). An example which might be examined briefly is the passage from page 47, line 16: 'Juste à ce moment' to page 48, line 5: 'j'ai répondu que non'. Here we have some of the most characteristic features of the principal tone Meursault adopts throughout the book: the use of the perfect tense for the specific events recounted and the present for reflection and general comment; a conversational register for most of the passage and a familiar register for dialogue: 'si c'est pas malheureux'. Sentences are short; ideas are linked, if at all, by the simplest constructions: *mais, et, d'ailleurs*. Verbal constructions predominate; adjectives are sparse, simple and concrete. The impression the passage gives is of a rather haphazard association of observations about Raymond; in no sense does it constitute a literary portrait. Critics have described this tone as that of an 'homme du peuple' (7, p. 98) or of a child (12, pp. 43-8). In this, as in so much else, Meursault appears to go against literary convention. In an interesting study, M.-G. Barrier has shown that the book is not entirely uniform in this respect: there are indeed signs of a much more formal, conventional style, as for example in the description of Pérez: 'ses cheveux blancs assez fins laissaient passer de curieuses oreilles ballantes et mal ourlées dont la couleur rouge sang dans ce visage blafard me frappa' (26), or of Pérez fainting at the funeral: 'on eût dit un pantin disloqué' (30-31). Barrier concludes that the elements of the neutral *écriture* are active and have the effect of neutralizing the 'literary' elements (9, p. 11). If indeed one examines further the passage under discussion, one finds that Meursault is quite aware that Raymond glosses over his more dubious activities, but is prepared to accept him as he is. Similarly, the passage reveals a conscious structuring: from general comment and rumour about Raymond, Meursault passes to his own response to him, which in turn leads to Meursault's observation of his physical appearance and an example of his speech; this all sets the scene for the continuance of the action with 'nous sommes montés'. Moreover the apparently colourless linking terms could be interpreted as being extremely precise. This is indicated in the opening phrase 'juste à ce moment'; the pauses marked by *pourtant, mais* and *d'ailleurs* suggest that the narrator is weighing up the order and the import of his statements; finally, if Meursault renounces other links apart from the anodine *et,* and prefers to break up the narrative into short sentences, it could well be to show that for him there is no necessary causal link between the independent statements. In other words, we have here a controlled and chosen neutrality.

This becomes clearer from examination of a passage which contains features of the second main tone of the novel, which is the adoption of an indirect or oblique vision. The passage from page 152 line 15: 'le fond de sa pensée' to page 153 line 20: 'en quelque sorte' is illustrative. In much of this passage Meursault is employing the 'style indirect libre', giving a paraphrase of the *procureur*'s arguments, but these are also given briefly in direct speech (152, lines 18-23). This passage in direct speech, short though it is, bears a highly structured, rhetorical stamp. The *doublement* of the first sentence creates a tight and inevitable link with the second sentence, and anticipates the emotive metaphor: 'l'aveuglante clarté des faits'. This rhetoric which, in strong contrast to the neutral tone, thrives on abstractions, does not disdain to descend to a lower register in the other extract quoted in direct speech: 'pour être sûr que la besogne était bien faite': for the *procureur,* all means are legitimate to secure condemnation. From 'j'avais écrit . . .' to the end of the passage, the *procureur*'s speech is reported by Meursault in indirect discourse. It is not without resemblance to Meursault's own neutral tone, with its short sentences and mainly verbal constructions, indeed in a sense it consciously apes Meursault's style in this and in appropriating the *je* form. But the heaviness of the pluperfects: 'je lui avais demandé . . . j'étais revenu . . . j'avais abattu . . .', firm and directional, contrasts with the lightness of touch, the near-transparency of Meursault's own perfects. Meursault transmits the *procureur*'s speech in a third manner: from page 152 line 23: 'il a résumé les faits' to page 153 line 2: 'la rentrée avec Marie'; adjudging the speech the status of fact, reporting directly, not obliquely. This short passage acts as a transition between the *procureur*'s statements and Meursault's own attitude at this point, which is characterized by naïvety. This is evident from the initial 'si j'ai bien compris', suggesting caution as to the interpretation of the *procureur*'s discourse; it is strongly brought out in 'j'ai mis du temps à le comprendre, à ce moment, parce qu'il disait "sa maîtresse" et pour moi, elle était Marie', where Meursault's apparent naïvety introduces a contrasting view to that of the *procureur;* finally, the closing 'en quelque sorte', Meursault's naïve appraisal of the *procureur*'s conclusion, has the effect of casting doubt on the whole process whereby the *procureur* has reached that conclusion. To sum up, it is through Meursault's neutrality of tone, which in this passage appears as naïvety, that the indirectness of the *procureur*'s speech is illuminated and at the same time questioned. The effects the *procureur* obtains, and the attitudes he represents, can only fully be appreciated by reference to a norm, and that norm is provided by Meursault's neutrality. In fact, since Meursault represents the antithesis of the *procureur,* he is not neutral at all, but arguing a different case. The means he employs is a calculated simplicity.

The third tone, which characterizes in particular the passage leading up to and describing the murder, seems to belie notions of neutrality and even calculated simplicity. If one looks at a short extract from page 94 line 24: 'je ne sentais plus que' to page 95 line 11: 'tout a commencé', one finds that the salient features are precisely the adjectives: *éclatant, brûlante, douloureux, épais, ardent,* and the metaphors 'les cymbales du soleil', 'le glaive éclatant jailli du couteau'. In fact the simplicity of the tone is continuing as before in the basic constructions Meursault continues to employ: 'cette épée brûlante rongeait mes cils et fouillait mes yeux douloureux. C'est alors que tout a vacillé. La mer a charrié un souffle épais et ardent', but it is overlaid by the metaphors which introduce greater complexity of perception and emotion. Now in the other two passages considered above, the neutral tone was in control. Describing Raymond and Meursault's attitude to him, the tone was harmonious, univocal. In the second passage there was duality of tone between the *procureur*'s reported speech and Meursault's reflections, but the neutral tone remained dominant, exploiting and puncturing the *procureur*'s discourse.

Here by contrast the neutral tone is pushed aside, the naïve simplicity appearing now as helplessness. As Meursault is no longer able to protect himself against the onslaught of the natural world, so Meursault's narrative is overcome by tumultuous language.

Thus the neutrality, or preferably the apparent simplicity of Meursault's tone, which appears in all three styles, corresponds to the operations of Meursault's consciousness. It is indeed a conscious tone, the result of a consistent effort to overcome two kinds of temptation. The first is the temptation to give way to intense poetic description, which would be the imaginative counterpart to his vibrant physical awareness; the second is to acquiesce in the twists and shifts of rhetoric and in abstraction. Meursault's adherence to the colourless monotone is both an illustration of these temptations and a revolt against facile expression; his tone is a constant tension.

This is perhaps the only solution, if expression is not to distort experience. Unless, of course, one remains silent; the book hints that language conveys only imperfectly the meaning intended: Céleste's sincere and despairing 'c'est un malheur' (142) comes across in the courtroom as banal and pathetic. Or if a verbal summary, however plausible, is made, it may miss or deny the truth of experience. This occurs both in the reconstruction of the murder and in the treatment of isolated pieces of evidence: 'Marie... a dit que ce n'était pas cela, qu'il y avait autre chose, qu'on la forçait à dire le contraire de ce qu'elle pensait' (145). Of course the trial is the verbal arena *par excellence,* and Meursault by contrast, privately, guards his silences jealously: 'le jour finissait et c'était l'heure dont je ne veux pas parler, l'heure sans nom' (126). Some sentiments are perhaps too precious to be half-expressed, and one thinks of Meursault's unexpressed grief for his mother, the silence between them as her gaze followed him around the flat.

But silence does not make a novel. While in one sense *L'Etranger* is so consistently distrustful of language, it is at the same time an act of faith in language. In its narration, it confirms the belief that different types of language can reveal and make explicit a range of attitudes, that the language of the novel is robust enough to sustain its own failings and tensions, and finally that the medium of language can transmit the intentions of protagonist, narrator and author.

5

La Chute: *Falling*

'Plus d'un, comme moi sans doute, écrivent pour
n'avoir plus de visage. Ne me demandez pas qui
je suis et ne me dites pas de rester le même'.

Michel Foucault, *L'Archéologie du savoir*

IN the introductory parallel Clamence draws with his interlocutor, he states: 'vous avez à peu près mon âge, l'œil
renseigné des quadragénaires qui ont à peu près fait le tour
des choses' (12-13). A man in middle life, then, the age at
which one surveys what has passed and prepares for what is
to come. As Clamence looks back to his past in Paris, he sees
a man at the peak of physical condition and performance, 'fait
pour avoir un corps' (32). But as the account of that past
progresses, so Clamence's physical health deteriorates. The
stages go from minor health troubles and depression (47),
through loss of coordination (84), pressing preoccupation with
death (95), to localized liver troubles and general fatigue
(111). The first crisis past, Clamence begins to accommodate
to and rationalize the ageing process: 'il ne s'agissait plus que
de vieillir' (114). A hard fact for a man like Clamence to face,
certainly, but worse is to come. The thought that ageing is a
peaceful, autumnal process turns out to be an illusion which is
shattered immediately as Clamence realizes that physical
decline is accompanied by regret and burning memories (115);
nostalgia for youth continues to haunt him (152).

All these events form part of Clamence's reconstructed
past. The present of the narration confirms that the decline
has not ceased. On first acquaintance Clamence gives the
impression of exuberance and vitality, perambulating freely in
Amsterdam. On the third day he confesses to not feeling on

form, to some respiratory difficulty (48); on the fourth day he describes his fatigue and a certain mental confusion (78); the fifth day finds him sitting in a deckchair on the boat (104) and shivering in the damp (118); by the sixth day fever has set in (145, 151), he receives his visitor lying down, and both his fatigue and his respiratory troubles have increased. In the course of the book there seems to be a clear fall from youth and health, accentuated towards the end.

What are we to make of this? Forty, these days, is still young, and Clamence shows no signs of dying — yet. Are we to believe his reassurance to the interlocutor not to alarm himself, since his delirium is directed, a part of the act? Clamence may like to think that he can simulate premature decline, but the unpalatable truth, and the truth of Clamence's past, remains: ageing is an irreversible process, followed by death. Clamence's simulation approximates to the facts, even though he has not got there yet. Possibly his acting out of the tragedy of life and death is an attempt to conjure fate, to delay the end; certainly he points to a truth of life, that man's existence is a continued fall from birth to death.

As Clamence falls into age, he falls into consciousness of self. Before looking at the depths to which he descends, it is instructive to consider from what point he fell. His physical well-being was matched by an edenic, perfect coincidence between himself and his life, in which his every reaction brought satisfaction, and every stimulus a coordinated response. In sum, it was a 'vie réussie' in mundane terms (32), otherwise expressed 'la vie en prise directe' (31).

Or was it? At the same time as arguing that man falls from innocence to guilt, as we shall discuss shortly, Clamence contrives to cast suspicion upon the very innocence from which he fell, by suggesting firstly that such a state is quite unthinkable in present-day French society: how could you hold hands with another man in a Paris street? and secondly, that even if it were possible, it might not be desirable. If we were to revert to a primitive state, wouldn't we all be *gorilles* anyway? And the *patron* of the Mexico-City bar hardly invites emulation. If

Clamence can discredit innocence, guilt will seem the more comfortable.

Three points punctuate Clamence's fall into consciousness: the laughter on the Pont des Arts (43), the body falling into the Seine from the Pont Royal (74-76) and the floating debris which Clamence mistakes for a corpse (114-15). Each of these points is followed by a phase during which Clamence reacts and adjusts to the new discovery.

The laughter, disembodied, suggests another reaction towards Clamence than his previous satisfaction and certainty; it breaks the unity and coherence of his life, introducing a double standard. The third chapter retraces the initial effect on Clamence: through reflection and memory he becomes increasingly aware of discrepancies between his actions and their underlying motivation, between *le paraître* and *l'être,* to the point at which he reaches 'le souvenir qui m'attendait' (56), the episode on the Pont Royal. This stage, catalysed by imagination and carried forward by mental activity, shows him clearly that the mind is double: behind the confident assessment waits its destructive counterpart, capable of negating all previous certainties.

The suicide takes the process of falling on to a different level; Clamence fails to help another human being, and the phase which follows, outlined in chapters four and five, is concerned with external, human contacts, the world outside the mind. Clamence is firstly concerned with the world of activity, contacts with men, whether friends, colleagues, associates. Appropriately, Clamence in this phase is more active, and he seeks to try to reestablish the harmony which his experiences have disrupted. When he surveys his associations with others, association tending to suggest community of interest, at the very least, he realizes that acceptance is in fact replaced by judgement (83). Judgement in itself implies separation of object and agent, the establishment of duality. In an effort to overcome this, Clamence seeks to appear in fact what he really is: to make *le paraître* again coincide with *l'être*. This he does through his real or imagined acts of aggressive behaviour, detailed at some length (96-101). Here, however, he meets with resistance compounded of incredulity and prejudice; others simply will not accept that he is as he appears; in the world, appearance and reality are separated.

So Clamence turns to more inward and intimate relationships with women. He experiences a need or lack, a dull suffering (105), which translates an aspiration towards union or unity, which he attempts to achieve through love. But he meets a double defeat; his egocentrism stands in the way of communion (107); the reality fails to coincide with the expectation: 'l'amour promis par les livres, et que je n'avais jamais rencontré dans la vie' (106-7). Through chastity, then, he endeavours to ignore the need; through debauchery to deaden it, and eventually reaches a plateau where aspiration and sensation are alike muffled: 'hors de mon métier enfin, je voyais peu de monde, entretenais la survie pénible d'une ou deux liaisons fatiguées' (114). This second phase, then, shows man divorced from himself, his ideals and his actions. Clamence could have saved the woman but he did not, from lethargy and from lack of will. This is the 'duplicité profonde de la créature' (90) which emerges from Clamence's essential discovery.

When Clamence mistakes the flotsam for a corpse, he falls again, for this experience bears out to him that nothing, henceforward, can be a mere piece of debris, nothing can be simple again, for the most concrete aspects of experience are overlaid with memories, imaginings, regrets. Experience itself is double, flawed. So the three experiences reveal to the fullest extent the duality of living and being, and Clamence's various attempts to reestablish unity fail absolutely.

His reaction is to try to accommodate to living in the *malconfort* (115), since there is no exit, and his conclusion, which he has proclaimed ever since, is that all are guilty. It is worth looking at what Clamence understands by guilt and innocence in this context. The state of innocence is the state prior to his fall, in which he coincided perfectly with his life, and from which judgement was absent: a state of unity. Guilt, conversely, is a state of discord, dissonance, duality, upon which judgement sets the seal by pronouncing and rendering it irreparable. Through his reflection and his experience man falls into consciousness of this state of estrangement.

It is appropriate to employ the word 'man', for Clamence presents this fall in ontological terms: he speaks of his 'découverte essentielle' (74) which occurred on the Pont *Royal:* the royal road, the true way. Further, Clamence puts forward his experiences as those of an Everyman which, with little dissemblance, happen to all. His fall is that of Adam, the first, archetypal man, and the fact that he is condemned, or has condemned himself, to repeat his fall *ad infinitum* with each new acquaintance, recalls Sisyphus and his eternal task.

Once again, however, the suspicion arises that Clamence has petrified his fall in order to prevent a further descent. To conclude — even on universal guilt — gives one something to hold on to, which may ward off further surprises and unpleasant experiences. And obsessive concern with one's past has at least the merit of diverting attention from the present. Clamence's main thesis is, one must admit, virtually unassailable: as Camus had noted long before, in *Le Mythe de Sisyphe:* 'commencer à penser, c'est commencer d'être miné' (*P2,* 100). This fall, like the ageing process, permits of no arrest.

The way in which the fall into consciousness is presented seems at first to approximate to the procedure of psychoanalysis, as Clamence's memory uncovers previously 'forgotten' incidents and he achieves new insights into himself. However the thrust of psychoanalysis is towards liberation of the individual through understanding and insight. The aim would be to dissolve a guilt complex, as the individual came to distinguish between a sense of shame for specific actions, and an unlocalized feeling of guilt. Clamence is concerned to present a permanent truth about human nature: that every one of us has committed shameful acts and is therefore guilty. Psychoanalysis suspends moral judgement and offers room for change; Clamence judges and prophesies: we have fallen, we will fall. His position is actually closer to that of the *moraliste* who uncovers layer upon layer of pretext masking the true motivation, which he then holds up for view: 'ce que les

hommes ont nommé amitié n'est qu'une société, qu'un ména-
gement réciproque d'intérêts, et qu'un échange de bons offices;
ce n'est enfin qu'un commerce où l'amour-propre se propose
toujours quelque chose à gagner'. [11] But again, while the
moraliste uncovers truths about human nature which are more
or less constant and predictable in all individuals, he too
abstains from moral judgement, describing but neither pre-
scribing nor condemning. Clamence needs both to judge and
to condemn; why is it that he cannot be satisfied with a mere
statement of fact? As Adèle King has noted, Clamence is 'an
individual who cannot live without clear moral absolutes' (*20*,
p. 660). He needs direction, as does modern man in general.
But his reiterated condemnations are those of someone who
would have liked things to be otherwise, who turns from *le
bien* to *le mal* just because *le bien* is not to be found, and who
is haunted by thoughts of purity while proclaiming universal
corruption.

Whilst being Everyman, Clamence is also to an extent a
portrait of Camus himself, and of the fall of a particular self-
image and image reflected by others. This aspect of the fall
will be treated in the chapter on context. Although Camus,
like his protagonist, would be unlikely to deny the auto-
biographical elements in the *récit,* he clearly intended it to
bear a more general significance, as is indicated both by a
provisional title Camus had in mind: *Un Héros de notre
temps,* and by the definitive *La Chute.*

If Clamence is a hero of our time, his fall is also that of
modern man, seen in a historical perspective. This is a fall
from one way of looking at the world to another, with all the
practical consequences. The state from which man has fallen
is a world-view based on secure and secured values: tolerance,
progress, freedom, the belief in intellectual, moral and social
development, which reached its apogee in the nineteenth
century. Behind these values lay the Christian ethic and the
belief in transcendence; the philosophy which complemented

---

[11] La Rochefoucauld, *Maximes,* in *Œuvres complètes* (Paris, Gallimard, 1964), p. 414.

and extended this view was the rational model, the belief that the world is accessible to reason and comprehensible to man. It is no accident that Clamence should be situated in Amsterdam, where Descartes, 'father of modern rationalism', wrote his *Discours de la méthode. La Chute* suggests clearly that rationalism is bankrupt, unable to meet the demands of a new age, in the same way as Descartes's former house has become a lunatic asylum (123).

Although Descartes's rationalism carried within itself the seeds of subversion of the very model it founded, modern man's fall is seen to take its clearest beginnings from Nietzsche's proclamation: 'God is dead'. For if God is dead, the values which sustain modern civilization collapse, and what is left? As we shall see later, Clamence's argument investigates the question of the death of the divinity, but he also explores the state of affairs on earth in the absence of a God and of philosophic certainty.

Lacking revealed truth, man attempts to manufacture certainty. This leads to totalitarian movements which replace the dialogue with the communiqué (50). Lacking belief in values, man gives free rein to his most bestial instincts, which find expression in concentration camps, the invention of the H-bomb, and the horrors of the Occupation and Resistance. Yet, one might argue, even if there are no eternal values or truths, is it not possible to found a relative humanism based on man? How, runs Clamence's answer, can one found anything on *homo duplex,* the creature who has imagined the tortures of the *malconfort* (116) and of the 'cellule des crachats' (117)? The Last Judgement is quite unnecessary, man's suffices; humanists today are café-habitués, scaredy-cats who jump at the name of God (98).

The common denominator in the strands of Clamence's exploration is that modern man cannot cope with his disorientation and freedom and seeks in 'isms' a relief from his responsibility and a refuge from his fear. This is the real problem: man was no better while God was alive; he traded in human lives, his imagination was equally diabolic. Man has become a frightened, vulnerable creature seeking salvation in seedy bars;

therefore, Clamence can be successful as a judge-penitent, offering assurance in a secular world.

It is difficult not to accept the general tenor of Clamence's argument; on the whole man is fragile, and the modern age has repulsive aspects. Yet against this one would want to set acts of self-abnegation, of courage and humanity. Clamence does indeed instance exceptions: the man who slept on the floor in order to share the discomfort of his imprisoned friend (36), the fact that there was a resistance movement organized against the Nazis. But no sooner mentioned, the examples are subsumed into the generality of Clamence's argument, drowned in the greater number of the multitude. Clamence's position depends on total assent: the exception threatens his security as judge-penitent and might, perhaps, recommence his fall.

There is a sense in which the fall may be said to go beyond previous descriptions to become a metaphysical question, a fall from total innocence to ultimate guilt. Now at first sight a metaphysical question is difficult to distinguish from an ontological one. Have we not used the same terms earlier, in describing man's ontological fall? At this point the meaning and context of the terms guilt and innocence have to be re-examined.

A metaphysical question is a type of 'end-question', one which pushes out as far as it can go, to deal with reality behind appearance. As S. N. Hampshire has noted: 'A systematic metaphysician need not speculate on the immortality of the soul; but he will always, I think, need to use some variant of ordinary language in a context in which the ordinary limitations of human experience are somehow removed.' [12] And if one probes this far, one reaches the stage of making statements which are not empirically verifiable. It would be possible, theoretically at least, to establish whether people experience the various kinds of estrangement we looked at earlier. Similarly, one could state which persons were in legal terms innocent or guilty of a particular offence. What it is not possible

---

[12] 'Metaphysical Systems' in *The Nature of Metaphysics,* edited by D. F. Pears (London, Macmillan, 1957), pp. 27-28.

to do is to demonstrate whether they are, simply and generally, innocent or guilty. When Clamence describes a fall from being in a state of harmony to being in a state of estrangement, he is talking in ontological terms; when he goes on to call this a fall from innocence to guilt, it becomes a question of metaphysics.

In the Western tradition it is Christian thought which is associated with questions of guilt and innocence in this sense, and one might wonder why Clamence, who proclaims himself 'pas chrétien pour un sou' (144) should share the preoccupations and the language of that faith. Thereby, perhaps, he will make man's fall appear the more definitive. To an audience which still lives partly according to a neo-Christian model, a presentation in Christian terms might secure ultimate conviction. Again, present-day society still functions on a worn Christian-based ethic which goes back long before the nineteenth, eighteenth and seventeenth centuries which Clamence passes under review. In order fully to expose the hypocrisy of that ethic, Clamence needs to attack it on its own terms: at source.

This might be sufficient answer, but I think that one needs to press further to account squarely for the fact that Christian associations pervade the book and inform its central preoccupations. Underlying Clamence's discourse are two concurrent and sustained hypotheses, each of which depends on a different role or figure that Clamence adopts.

The first hypothesis assumes Christianity as it has been revealed, and looks at three principal areas in which it might be challenged: the dogma, the ethic, and the community of the faithful. Here Clamence adopts the role of the last prophet, John the Baptist, as suggested both by his Christian name, Jean-Baptiste, and by the clear association with the 'vox clamans in deserto', the voice crying in the wilderness.

On the level of dogma, that which essentially distinguishes Christ from a prophet is his divinity: he is not simply a 'friend of God', he is God, made man. Further, what distinguishes the incarnate God from his creatures in his sinlessness, earthly manifestation of divine perfection. According to Clamence,

Christ is indirectly responsible for the murder of the innocents, therefore he is in fact guilty. So he may be a remarkable human being, but he is not God. The ethic should follow from the dogma, but if Christ is guilty, this casts doubt upon any ideals of purity or innocence which are based upon the model he gave. Religion, which proposes the model of Christ to man, is therefore seen as an 'entreprise de blanchissage' (118), dishonest both intellectually and morally. As for the faithful, who should be witnesses to their faith, no experiential evidence assures Clamence of the desirability of being a Christian (55, 121), nor does anything but the appellation appear to distinguish Christians from other human beings.

Clamence seems to be suggesting that it is more honest, as well as more realistic, to admit the hollowness of Christian pretensions, even if that means that one is left with the sort of world in which Clamence reigns supreme. Once again one might wish to take issue at this point. Christian dogma makes it quite clear that Christ bore the sin of the world, even though it holds that he was personally innocent of moral evil. The words from the cross: 'My God, my God, why hast thou forsaken me?' [13] clearly point to the estrangement from God which the burden of sin effects. Secondly, although societal ethic is based on neo-Christian values, the attitude of Christ was one of transformation of existing values, as when he cleansed the temple of the moneylenders. [14] Thirdly, although the Christian is exhorted and expected to be a living example of his faith, the revelation of, appropriately, St. John the Divine contains a far more stringent condemnation of the mediocre than that which Clamence offers: 'How I wish you were either hot or cold: But because you are lukewarm, neither hot nor cold, I will spit you out of my mouth'. [15] So Clamence is either biased or misinformed. He is concerned to effect the downfall of Christianity, for he cannot accept that the Christian way of looking at the world alters the categories

---

[13] Matthew XXVII. 46.
[14] Matthew XXI. 12-13.
[15] Revelation III. 16-17.

we normally recognize, and that faith re-evaluates and trans-
forms existing data. Clamence wants to be able to say that
something is either divine or human, innocent or guilty, pure
or hypocritical, admirable or worthy of condemnation.

The second hypothesis is that God is dead, and that therefore Christianity is confounded. If God does not exist, then
Clamence is God, Alpha and Omega, the definitive Judge:
'Heureusement, je suis arrivé, moi! Je suis la fin et le commen-
cement, j'annonce la loi. Bref, je suis juge-pénitent' (124). By
extension, Clamence is Christ, and aspects of Clamence's life
can be seen as a pitiable, parodic simulation of Christ's agony
and passion: the continued fall a species of *via dolorosa,* the
attendant women, including the prostitute, the blow during
the traffic incident (58), Clamence's talk to the group of young
lawyers and their bafflement (99-101), recalling the disciples'
incomprehension at Christ's death, the appeal 'il faut me pardonner ces imprudences; je ne savais pas ce que je faisais'
(141) for 'Father, forgive them, for they know not what they
do'. [16] In similar, unworthy form, Clamence takes on the third
person of the Trinity, but as a spirit who cannot get the doves
to descend on the heads of men and who, unable to breathe
the breath of life, suffers from respiratory troubles. Phan Thi
Ngoc-Mai and Pierre Nguyen Van-Huy have suggested an
identification between Clamence and Lucifer (*21,* pp. 147-
171), and indeed if God is dead and Clamence becomes God,
so also he becomes the devil. The fall is also then the fall of
the Archangel. Clamence explicitly takes on the role of the
Pope, vicar of Christ on earth, successor of Peter to whom
Christ gave the keys of heaven and hell. One may also, as
P-L. Rey has noted (*23,* p. 53), see in Clamence an anti-
Christ, the Christ of the days when there shall be wars and
rumours of wars, not only the prophet, but the saviour of
modern times.

So Clamence's immense ego takes on a six-fold dimension,
an unholy double trinity of form. This seems a somewhat
precarious solution; it may afford him personal satisfaction,

---

[16] Luke XXIII. 34.

but is hardly likely to be acceptable even to his converts. How does he attempt to convince his hearers of the irrelevance, if not the nullity, of Christian beliefs? This brings us on to a further, and final, way of interpreting the fall.

In this interpretation, Clamence does not argue against the Christian possibility: his endeavour is to reduce the status of the fall, to demystify it and strip it of its resonance, and this in two areas and in two ways: he attempts to show the fall in concrete, everyday terms, and he shows it, alternatively, as simply a literary myth.

Men tend to continue to speak in a particular idiom long after the model which inspired it has been disproved or rejected. As regards Christianity, if people really believe that the divinity has been replaced by man, they have no business to shudder at God's name. Here Clamence carries out a certain exorcism, showing up areas of particular sensitivity in which one might be tempted to go along with religious associations, and prompting the interlocutor or reader to ask why, in a secular world, one should do this. For after all, in the book, the fall is a body falling into the Seine, hell is Amsterdam, 'the Pope' a charade enacted by J.-B. Clamence. Why should they be any more than that? If one is realistic, this is the only way of interpreting these contaminating terms.

The second aspect of Clamence's demystification attempts to carry the exorcism backwards in time. Some of the most acute sensibilities in the Western intellectual tradition: Dante, Pascal, Dostoievsky, to name but three of those who have contributed to *La Chute,* have devoted their power and their vision to the restatement of the Christian truth. Clamence is aware that an effective way of neutralizing the force of such visions is to reduce them to the status of cultural allusion and focus on the criterion of literary excellence. His allusion to Dante's last circle of hell, followed by the exclamation: 'Vous savez cela? Diable, vous devenez plus difficile à classer' (19), effectively cuts short any enquiry the interlocutor might have made into the real relevance of Dante's vision to the modern world; Clamence obliges him to accept the Dantesque parallel he, Clamence, has already provided. In Clamence's presentation of Amsterdam in terms of Dante's hell, and himself as guide, the sense of awe and mystery in Dante has given way, for the reader, to intellectual curiosity to see how the literary parallel will be sustained. Similarly, by simulating Pascal's arguments for Christianity and attempting to refute them, Clamence draws attention away from Pascal's central, and disturbing thesis, namely that rational argument cannot bring one to the Christian truth: only the wager of faith is relevant.

So Christianity may live on as a literary myth, but without essential significance. Man will have no need of it in everyday terms. If he still needs a myth, let him create one, as Clamence has created his own of replacing the Trinity; if he finds support in literary myth, *La Chute* has provided a further layer of myth: the reader is tainted, henceforward, for evocations of the fall will be inseparable from the story of Clamence.

It is difficult not to admire a certain stringency in Clamence's criticism, the condemnation of hypocrisy and a sensitivity to the temptation of going along with, or sliding into, Christianity for aesthetic reasons or for lack of questioning. But again, doubt strikes as to the convincingness of Clamence's argument. The fact that he attempts to emasculate Christian thought suggests that he is aware of its challenge to his position; although the fall may be a splash in the water, it continues to haunt him, whether for psychological or other reasons. It would seem that in this sense also, Clamence portrays the fall in such a way as to stop falling himself.

In all the senses of the fall we have examined, one is inclined to accept much of the main argument which Clamence is putting forward. In each case, however, there is the hint of a contrary argument, and the substance of his discourse appears to be an attempt to secure himself and the position he has chosen to represent. The content of Clamence's preaching is, however, only half the story; it depends in its turn on the manner and the direction of his speech.

6

La Chute: *Roles*

'ceux qui ont été longtemps bons avocats ne sont
pas pour cela meilleurs juges'.

Descartes, *Discours de la méthode*

CLAMENCE's discourse is conditioned by the four different
principal roles he adopts. We know that he has been a
lawyer in Paris, but it is easy to forget that he continues to
exercise his former profession sporadically in Amsterdam
(44). Now in an extremely simplified way, the profession of
lawyer might be described as twofold: in particular, to argue
a case, and in general, to practise the law. As Clamence admits, to argue a case the discourse must be directed: 'mon
discours est orienté' (139). This aim will affect both the content and the form of the plea; it means that evidence which
is not relevant to the argument will be left aside; it means that
the discourse itself, to convince, will obey certain conventions:
logic, rational argument, appeal to empirical evidence. Secondly, the law must be respected. From this it follows that
the exception must be accommodated into the general *corpus,*
and that expression will be directed into channels of generality; from this Clamence derives his licence to practise the
magisterial statement: 'la vérité est que tout homme intel-
ligent, vous le savez bien, rêve d'être un gangster et de régner
sur la société par la seule violence' (60).

After having been a lawyer Clamence becomes a judge,
and a judge-penitent. The profession of judge might be seen
as the culmination of the legal process and career in the same
way as becoming a judge-penitent is the apex of Clamence's
experiences. For the judge pronounces the sentence after consideration of the pleas submitted by the lawyers. The im-

portant thing is that the judge must pronounce, one way or another. The calling of judge-penitent again implies necessary judgement, with the added proviso that the judge-penitent must secure the confession of his client: there is no place in his system for a verdict of not guilty. The statements Clamence makes in his role of judge are summary, definitive judgements: on modern man: 'il forniquait et lisait des journaux' (11); on the individual: 'ça fait tant. Vous êtes un pervers, un satyre, un mythomane, un pédéraste, un artiste, etc.' (140).

So consideration of Clamence's twin legal roles reveals to what extent his discourse is necessarily orientated by the nature of the role. It shows, furthermore, that a conclusion is inevitable, and a particular type of conclusion. There is no room, within these roles, for saying 'perhaps' or 'but', for putting forward anything other than the argument, or for suspending judgement. And how could one appeal to beauty, to faith, or to poetry? Fortunately, there are other approaches to experience than the legal, other professions than that of lawyer.

Compared with the definitive formulae of the legal roles, the third *persona* Clamence adopts seems to point in a rather different direction. In the conversation about the *enseigne* individuals might choose to proclaim their calling, Clamence envisages his visiting cards printed with 'Jean-Baptiste Clamence, comédien' (52). He mentions in passing that he has indeed done some acting in the army (66, 93) and has already played numerous roles or scenes in his private life (66). Clamence's talent in this direction is revealed in the ease with which he picks up the remarks or gestures of his interlocutor and carries them forward, presenting them, as it were, on the stage of his discourse. This can be seen in the Dante reference quoted above (p. 61) and in the example discussed later (pp. 78-79). Moreover, the book presents Clamence in various poses or scenes: Clamence in the Mexico-City bar, Clamence on board ship, Clamence receiving his visitor, Clamence as 'Elie sans messie, bourré de fièvre et d'alcool, le dos collé à cette porte moisie, le doigt levé vers un ciel bas, couvrant d'imprécations des hommes sans loi qui ne peuvent supporter aucun jugement' (124). One cannot but admire the extent of his range, which comprises the confidential whisper, the whimsical musing, the sly wink, the moment of exaltation. The language of Clamence's role of actor is in itself transparent: there is no particular type of statement which can be described as characteristic of the actor, but this role is responsible for the variety of tone and colour which pervades his whole discourse. We do not know the real name of Clamence; so, an actor might be said to be characterized by dispersion: he is defined by the different roles he plays, none of which corresponds to himself. How do we interpret Clamence as actor? Should we conclude that Clamence is really elsewhere, not fully accounted for by any of the roles he plays, in the same way as the actor's personality is distinct from his parts? Or should we take it that Clamence is playing some of an indefinite number of roles, which the reader himself can choose and perform? Either alternative would confirm that the book itself, and Clamence's argument, are 'à prendre ou à laisser' (8); it depends whether we find Clamence convincing in his roles, whether we are persuaded by his arguments.

Clamence's fourth main role, that of John the Baptist, has been mentioned earlier but merits further study as it is played throughout the book. In many respects Clamence simulated John's career: John was a latter-day prophet, the last in the line before the Messiah, who lived in the desert, clothed in camel's hair, and baptized with water. [17] Clamence, prophet of modern times, clad in his camel-hair coat, lives in Amsterdam surrounded by the water of the canals and the rain, and travels on the Zuyderzee. John was executed and his head displayed on a platter; Clamence visualizes the same end, the head shown to the people (154-55). Clamence appropriates the language of prophecy to proclaim the inevitability of judgement and to present a vision of the apotheosis: 'Je trône parmi mes vilains anges, à la cime du ciel hollandais,

---

[17] For the career of John the Baptist, see Matthew III, XI and XIV.

je regarde monter vers moi, sortant des brumes et de l'eau, la multitude du Jugement dernier' (151). It is by prophetic licence that he perfects the denunciatory diatribe: 'Ah! les petits sournois, comédiens, hypocrites, si touchants avec ça! Croyez-moi, ils en sont tous, même quand ils incendient le ciel. Qu'ils soient athées ou dévots, moscovites ou bostoniens, tous chrétiens, de père en fils' (143).

But in spite of the superficial and claimed resemblance, profound distinctions separate Clamence from John the Baptist. Traditionally the prophet revivifies religion; Clamence preaches its demise. The prophets point to another, the Messiah who will be revealed; Clamence's finger points to himself and to his interlocutor. John proclaimed his inferiority compared to Christ; Clamence gloats and exults. John, in spite of being contemporary with and related to Christ, doubted, at the end, whether he really was the Messiah, and sent disciples to ask for reassurance; Clamence's whole effort is directed towards stifling doubt and 'le rire'. Clamence may be a prophet appropriate to the age, but once more it is up to the reader whether he takes him for a true prophet, a false prophet, or for a prophet who is true so far as he goes, but whose role is to be a precursor; who shows up the inadequacy of what he offers by comparison with what is to come, and whose only justification is to announce something else.

If there is something else which runs counter to Clamence's argument, judgement and prophecies, is it even hinted at in the book? It is clear that Clamence in his earlier life was dissatisfied: 'il me semblait, à l'extrémité de la fatigue, et l'espace d'une seconde, que je comprenais enfin le secret des êtres et du monde. Mais la fatigue disparaissait le lendemain et, avec elle, le secret; je m'élançais de nouveau. Je courais ainsi, toujours comblé, jamais rassasié' (34). In his present existence, in spite of his protestations to the contrary, he is still unhappy, still menaced by doubt and the outbreak of laughter: 'Parfois, de loin en loin, quand la nuit est vraiment belle, j'entends un rire lointain, je doute à nouveau' (150). His preaching, his presentation of the fall, are designed to save himself. But how much further down could Clamence go? What would he save himself from? From the obscure conviction that there is a 'secret des êtres et du monde' to which beauty, nature, friendship, point the way, but to which he can never accede. Since he cannot enter into the kingdom, it is better to pretend that it does not exist, and to content oneself with the exile. So Clamence deflates and brushes aside notions of innocence, youth, the beauty of the Greek islands. But he still cannot help seeing beauty even in the Dutch canals and snow, he cannot help appreciating the *Juges intègres*. Even if he flees to the far corner of Europe, even if he locks the picture away, he is still pursued, but no-one will ever come to arrest him and make everything plain. If he were tempted to think that the world could be beautiful or that people might sleep on the floor for their friends, how could he rely on such fragile indications, argue for them, reconcile them with the general picture of desolation? So Clamence locks them out, even though this gives him a 'complexe du verrou' (135). Perhaps the final irony in the roles of Clamence is that he chooses to bear witness in the world he portrays, ignoring the kingdom he glimpses, and becomes a prophet at the cost of remaining a traitor.

7

La Chute: *Structure*

> 'il faut que le lecteur invente tout dans un perpé-
> tuel dépassement de la chose écrite'.
>
> Sartre, *Qu'est-ce que la Littérature?*

THE six chapters of the book are divided at the central point by Clamence's 'découverte essentielle' occurring at the end of chapter three. This arrangement is of course calculated, since Clamence chooses to site his discovery at that point in the narrative, but the break does provide a two-part model of before and after the fall, with which both he and we can work.

However the structure of the book also acts as a corrective to any over-simplified or over-precise view of the fall, by presenting itself as a slow, unbroken fall throughout. Broadly, in the first chapter Clamence appears full of energy, a witty, entertaining companion, as he may well have appeared before the fall. The second chapter narrates events preceding the laughter on the Pont des Arts; the third chapter probes through successive layers behind which is revealed the episode of the suicide; the fourth chapter treats the outward and visible signs of Clamence's fall, the fifth the inward agitation. The sixth resumes Clamence's coming to terms with the situation in becoming a judge-penitent. This presentation too is structured by Clamence's mind and designed to convince.

Elements within the overall structure reveal a number of polarities which weave the theme of duality into the texture of the book. Clamence's love of heights and dominating situations contrasts with his claustrophobia and aversion to anything connected with the underground depths (28-29), from potholes to the Resistance. Hovering contrasts with falling (34, 109), the dry brightness of Greece with the grey mists of Holland, island summers with Dutch autumn and winter, light with dark, south with north. Spatially there appear to be three terms: the islands, Paris, Amsterdam, which correspond to different notions of temporality: the islands to a far-off past, a kind of pluperfect, Paris to the past and Amsterdam to the present. Effectively, though, Clamence works on a binary opposition of past and present, Paris and Amsterdam. At first sight Clamence's past, as he presents it, appears fixed and unalterable, while the present retains a certain fluidity as the venue of the daily conversations varies. But one soon realizes that Clamence is actually guiding his interlocutor round the city: leaving him purposely, at the end of chapter one, in front of the temptation of the red-light district, leading him gradually and inevitably to his door and finally inviting him inside. As the circle of the present tightens, so in a sense the grip of the past relaxes, in that one realizes that Clamence is manipulating events in his past like counters in a game, and that there is no necessary order to them: what counts is that he should win. The book contains, not so much fixed oppositions as an interplay of elements and the patterns and tensions of relationship which are thereby created. Truth and falsehood, for example, are not in perpetual opposition, but combine to move in a direction which illustrates a more general, perhaps deeper truth. Obviously Clamence has not really got the *Juges intègres* in his room, so he is lying about the way he obtained it; but the double fictional lie serves to lead one to reflect on the theme of appearance on show and reality hidden.

We have discussed at some length Clamence's relationship to himself, his life and his argument; it remains to look at some of the elements in the book which form, as it were, the background on which Clamence weaves his pattern. The narrative embraces a number of episodes involving a larger number of actors. In some of these Clamence is involved centrally as a participant, as in the traffic incident, or his reign as pope, in others he figures as an observer, as in the

story of the death and funeral of his *concierge;* other episodes
again are independent of Clamence personally, or affect him
in the sense that they narrate incidents from contemporary
history: the war and occupation. All types and conditions of
men and women people Clamence's episodes, giving a sense
of substance to the world he portrays. In the same way as the
Mexico-City bar appears as a microcosm of human life, so
Clamence's verbal excursions into the world tend to authen-
ticate his claim that he has seen life, is properly qualified to
assess what he has seen, and makes his assessment on the
basis of varied, thought-through experience.

Two examples may serve to illustrate Clamence's method
in introducing these episodes into his narrative, and the functions they might fulfill. The episode of the little Frenchman
who, at Buchenwald, proclaimed his innocence (86), claims a
certain independent life apart from Clamence's personal experiences, but like most examples evinced in conversation, tends
to reinforce a defined point of view. The humour of the incident springs from the disparity between the man's expectations
associated with innocence — that he would be listened to and
treated accordingly — and the reality which makes innocence
totally irrelevant. Clamence suggests that it is equally ridic-
ulous for us to claim innocence when reflection reveals guilt,
but that is not quite the same thing. The Frenchman's protest
may have been ineffectual, but his moral reflex was sound.
Everyone may have laughed, but if the parallel is exact, Clamence exhorts us to moral turpitude.

Another war story, that of 'Duguesclin' (132-33), provides
similar material. Clamence dictates the way in which he
intends the story to be taken with his interjection: 'Oui! c'est
un conte de fées, décidément'. In the first part of the story
Clamence plays little part, merely relating how 'Duguesclin'
came to suggest the election of a new pope. Clamence draws the
implicit moral on the ridicule of electing a man like himself
pope, which invites us to speculate on the degradation of the
papacy. 'Duguesclin' appears to have experienced a fall not
unlike Clamence's own: disillusioned by experience from expectations of moral and religious integrity, he conforms to

pragmatic reality by basing the new order on the weakness of man. But if the pope should fail, does that discredit all notion of holiness? If reality does not conform to expectations, must the hope and expectation always be jettisoned? One cannot base an argument on expectations, nor can one prove whether Clamence is consciously leaving an opening for disagreement. It would seem, however, that Camus intended the episode to point both ways.

A similar function to that performed by the episodes is fulfilled by the often extended literary allusions, with the difference that while the episodes effect a widening-out on the spatial plane, the allusions operate on a temporal continuum, linking Clamence's discourse with preceding intellectual tradition. Although many literary echoes reverberate throughout the book, [18] perhaps the most sustained allusions are those to Dante and to Descartes. [19]

Descartes's intellectual starting point was discontent with the learning in which he had been immersed and which seemed to him unable adequately to account for experience and provide him with certainty. Accordingly he spent the rest of his youth travelling and reading 'le grand livre du monde'. [20] He settled in Holland where he wrote the *Discours de la méthode*. The seeds of doubt were sown in Clamence by the laughter; after realizing that he would never escape from this condition he left Paris, travelled and settled in Amsterdam (146). Descartes's method is founded on universal doubt and seeks through reason and evidence to attain to certainty. The perfection of God is a guarantee that what we perceive clearly and distinctly is true. For Descartes, the world is ultimately knowable through reason; since reason is inherent in all, the

---

[18] In spite of the *caveats* outlined in the introduction, one may perhaps mention here Camus's stated indebtedness to Molière, and *Dom Juan* particularly, as one of his sources for *La Chute,* and in addition refer to the fact that over the period of genesis of *La Chute,* Camus was adapting Dostoievsky's *The Possessed* and Faulkner's *Requiem for a Nun.*

[19] Adèle King's study explores how the formal structure of *La Chute* is parallel to Dante's *Inferno* (20).

[20] *Discours de la méthode* (Paris, Garnier, 1960), p. 40.

method which he as an individual elaborated may be used by others, for experience taught him that he might 'juger par moi de tous les autres'. [21] The similarities with Clamence's method are obvious: the reasoning on the basis of universal guilt to reach certainty, the generalizing outwards. But Clamence's discourse clearly shows that reason cannot tell us what is true or false; it is not God but the absence of God which establishes Clamence's position.

Clamence follows his literary predecessors up to a point and then his discourse diverges. This casts a certain suspicion upon the good faith of the literary allusion, a hint which is reinforced by the fact that the laughter was heard on the Pont des *Arts* and that Clamence himself admits a degree of confusion between the discourse and its sources: 'ai-je lu cela ou l'ai-je pensé?' (71). It is not therefore surprising to find a non-verbal art, painting, employed also as an extended metaphor. The references to painting are numerous: Rembrandt's *Anatomy Lesson* (17), Gauguin dying 'fou et heureux' (18), a Vermeer interior (128), the Dutch specialization in tulips and pictures (44). But the most significant reference is to the panel *The Just Judges* which formed part of the Ghent altarpiece *The Adoration of the Mystic Lamb*. This theme is introduced at the beginning of the book (9) and repeated at greater length in the closing chapter (136-38); it therefore acts as a frame to the work. The notion of a frame, however, implies externality, whereas the *Just Judges* is also an extended metaphor, a parable even, which sums up, in miniature and non-verbally, the major themes of *La Chute*.

A brief excursion into the circumstances of the painting may illuminate how integrally the metaphor is woven into the work as a whole. The complete Ghent altarpiece, sculpture and painting, has been thought to be the work of *two* masters, Hubert and Jan Van Eyck; the painting is a polyptych composed of panels painted on *both* sides, so that the altarpiece presents one appearance when closed and another when open. In the nineteenth century the Berlin museum had the

---

21 Ibid., p. 36.

ingenious idea of having the outer panels sawn in *two,* enabling the whole composition ,to be taken in at a glance. The panel of the *Just Judges* depicts on the other side, John the Baptist. In 1934, as Clamence relates, this *double* panel was stolen; the thief replaced *John the Baptist,* holding the *Just Judges* for ransom, but the ransom money was so long in coming that the thief died, and the *Just Judges* panel remains unrecovered (my italics). As Jose Barchilon has noted: '*The Mystic Lamb* described the Vision of St John (the Evangelist) in the *Book of Revelation* (VII, 9-17), the text of which is *sung* by the subdeacon *at mass at the Feast of All Saints*' (*19,* p. 233) (his italics). So the metaphor acts as a cristallization: resuming in itself the theme of duplicity, and at the same time pointing beyond itself, inviting the reader to ponder upon the judges held for ransom and the juxtaposition of John the Baptist and John the Apostle. Yet concurrently, the picture leaves a blank space in the Mexico-City bar, and here the theme of the theft of the picture is integrated into the work to generate yet another question. What filled the empty space? This too relates to the orientation of *La Chute:* those who are washed up at the Mexico-City are confronted with a blank. They may choose to accept the picture Clamence draws, or they may substitute their own design.

This leads on to the problem of the interlocutor. Who is this man whom Clamence addresses and who accompanies him throughout the work? The question is, appropriately, twofold, concerned both with the *persona* of the interlocutor and with his response to Clamence. Critical opinion is divided as to whether the interlocutor accepts or rejects what Clamence proposes. I feel, however, that Camus has deliberately created such ambiguity as to make it virtually impossible to decide one way or another. The interlocutor seems to speak or interject less frequently, perhaps, as the book proceeds, but this does not mean that he acquiesces eventually. Similarly, the profession of the interlocutor accentuates the ambiguity of the conclusion. Before finally deciding on the profession of lawyer, Camus had earlier thought to make the interlocutor a children's magistrate or a policeman. To have done this would have

placed the emphasis in the first case on judgement, and in the
second on arrest. The profession of the interlocutor would
have led him to act predictably after listening to Clamence.
By contrast, if the interlocutor is a lawyer, he is free to
choose his argument. The ending Camus finally chose allows
for another possibility of interpretation: that the interlocutor
as such does not exist, but is merely Clamence's *alter ego.*
Clamence would therefore be trying to convince himself.
Thirdly, if the interlocutor is someone like Clamence, but
someone whose response is not predictable, this leaves the
greater latitude for identification of the interlocutor with the
reader. The more transparent the interlocutor, the more
directly Clamence seems to be addressing us; the more the
interlocutor approximates to Clamence, the more easily Clamence can intend his remarks for the 'hypocrite lecteur, mon
semblable, mon frère'.

The structure of the work in its turn echoes the themes
revealed in Clamence's discourse: duplicity and duality, the
attempt to convince, the ambiguity of statement and conclusion.
Detail of metaphor and incident is woven into the fabric of
the whole, creating a tautness of structure, confirming in-
divisibility of content and form.

8

La Chute: *Form and Style*

> 'In the case of despair ... being is related to the
> ability to be as a fall. Infinite as is the advantage
> of the possibility, just so great is the measure of
> the fall'.
>
> Kierkegaard, *The Sickness unto Death*

LA CHUTE is described not as a novel but as a *récit*. This
distinction does not depend purely on length: there is
little difference volume-wise between *La Chute* and *L'Etranger*, yet *L'Etranger* is described as a *roman*. P.-L. Rey in his
study of *La Chute* has an interesting discussion where he
quotes Gide's definition:

> un récit reproduit des événements conformément aux
> lois de l'exposition, un roman nous montre ces événe-
> ments dans leur ordre propre. ... Nous pouvons, aidés
> par cette formule, distinguer à grands traits le roman
> pur du récit pur; le roman a lieu, le récit a eu lieu; le
> roman vous livre peu à peu un caractère, le récit l'ex-
> plique; le roman regarde naître les événements, le récit
> les fait connaître; le roman est constitué par des suites
> vivantes, le récit par des causales; le roman se déroule
> au présent, le récit éclaire le passé.

On this basis Rey concludes that *L'Etranger* is a *roman* in
so far as 'Meursault est un personnage "en devenir"'; il raconte
sa propre histoire dans son "surgissement perpétuel", découvrant le monde et se découvrant lui-même, chapitre après
chapitre'. But Clamence 'ne subit aucune modification semblable au cours du récit. Il n'expose pas son passé de manière
à le revivre ou à le faire revivre dans son surgissement, mais
de manière à le faire comprendre' (*23*, p. 32).

This distinction is helpful to distinguish formally between the two works, and on the whole is justifiable. But one should not forget, as B. T. Fitch has pointed out, that in the case of *La Chute, récit* and *œuvre* are identical (*6,* p. 231), as indeed were *roman* and *œuvre* in the case of *L'Etranger.* It is not remarkable for the novel, which as a *genre* creates its own world; we expect, however, that a *récit* should make explicit that it is a *récit,* either by employing some device such as an editor's introduction or simply by being inserted in a *recueil* or collection of short stories. The story of Clamence's fall is in fact a *récit* inside *La Chute* which is itself a *récit*. Within the story of Clamence's fall again, as we have seen, are the episodes, in themselves miniature, illustrative stories, which all lead back to the dominant image of the fall. The work reminds one of the Russian wooden dolls, which when opened contain another smaller doll, and so on *ad parvissimam.*

But what of the framework, Clamence's meetings with the interlocutor which contain the *récit* of the fall? I would tend to agree with Rey that Clamence does not develop in the course of the work; to this extent one may agree that *La Chute* is formally a *récit.* But the aspect of *devenir* is implicit in the text: because it is directed to the interlocutor or reader, there is a gap between what Clamence says and the response of the hearer or reader which carries with it a developmental sense. Whether Clamence's argument is accepted or rejected, it reverberates beyond the spoken or written text, demanding reaction.

Clamence, like Meursault, employs the first person. In contrast to Meursault's distance from the reader, Clamence's *je* appears intrusively close. In this way familiarity with the protagonist tends to slide over into complicity and collusion, enabling Clamence to effect the passage from *je* to *nous* and, ultimately, to denounce the *vous.* But like Meursault's, Clamence's *je* is disturbing. For all its incessant repetition, we do not really grasp it; it is not anchored solidly in a constant *persona,* protagonist or hero. As we have seen, Clamence adopts a number of roles, and *je* is used for each of these in turn. Or again, when Clamence sees himself as the trinity, the *je* encapsulates three persons in one. If this were not enough, the *je* is splintered further by Clamence's extreme self-consciousness. When he states 'je plaide' (18), 'je deviens lyrique' (104), 'je crains de m'être exalté' (152), the absent *je* of the nameless narrator is observing J.-B. Clamence, actor, in his roles as lawyer, Romantic and prophet.

Unlike Meursault whose axis was primarily the perfect and the present, Clamence ranges through the whole gamut of tenses and moods, as his empire extends over all time. While the appeal to different tenses normally creates a sense of space in the narrative, Clamence uses tenses to extend his domination, and as one would expect, there is nothing fortuitous in his choice of tense. The stages in Clamence's fall and the episodes relating to them are delimited by the past historic, which clearly indicates their belonging to time past. Within this framework, the imperfect serves for reflection and comment. The model of past historic/imperfect characterizes that part of the work which Clamence holds up for show as comprising his story. [22] The perfect tense is employed to give a sense of greater diffuseness; it acts as a mediator between the events in Clamence's fall and the present of the narrative. I remarked with reference to *L'Etranger* on the open-ended nature of the perfect as compared with the past historic (p. 44). Clamence utilizes this association to considerable effect, allowing the perfect to suggest freedom, while in fact he is presenting the present as inevitably formed by, and repeating, the past. In the same sense, the obvious use of the present tense for the present of the narrative suggests a gap of spontaneity and free choice, but this appears as illusory when one considers how Clamence uses the future in a dominating and determining sense: 'J'écouterai, soyez-en sûr, votre propre confession . . . vous y viendrez, c'est inévitable . . . J'attendrai maintenant que vous m'écriviez ou que vous reveniez. Car vous reviendrez, j'en suis sûr! Vous me trouverez inchangé' (149). The conditional might seem by its nature unas-

---

[22] A most interesting structural study of the tenses and episodes has been made by Morten Nøjgaard (*22*).

sailable, and indeed Clamence allows it a certain non-determining latitude: 'pensez un peu à ce que serait votre enseigne' (52). But the interlocutor's seeming freedom to choose is overridden by the necessity of there being, as Clamence states, some *enseigne* which is appropriate. Elsewhere, Clamence capitalizes on the indeterminacy of the conditional to present a triumphant hypothesis: if there is conditionality, he has already anticipated it: 'Vous m'arrêteriez donc, ce serait un bon début. Peut-être s'occuperait-on ensuite du reste, on me décapiterait, par exemple, et je n'aurais plus peur de mourir, je serais sauvé. Au-dessus du peuple assemblé, vous élèveriez alors ma tête encore fraîche . . . Tout serait consommé, j'aurais achevé, ni vu ni connu, ma carrière de faux prophète qui crie dans le désert et refuse d'en sortir' (154-55).

A more detailed examination of particular passages may give substance to general remarks and illuminate Clamence's specific procedures. The paragraph on page 49 beginning 'Délicieuse maison, n'est-ce pas?' shows Clamence in his role as guide, introducing a new topic of conversation with a reference to the façade they happen to be passing. He invites the interlocutor to be horrified at the open and generalized abuse of human freedom, appealing to liberal, humanitarian sentiments. But even before he exclaims: 'Quel scandale!' Clamence has already subtly changed the object of his indignation. His reference to his Parisian colleagues appears to confirm the initial impression, for they too condemn slavery. However the end of the paragraph completes the ironic *volte-face:* the scandal is not that slavery exists, but that it is admitted to exist. The ironic structure of the paragraph enables Clamence to express a further level of irony at the expense of so-called liberals. The relationship of this paragraph to the following pages illustrates how themes in *La Chute* are continually interrelated and intertwined. Immediately following this paragraph Clamence continues the theme of slavery and domination, but the theme of the *enseigne* is reintroduced on page 52: just suppose everyone had one, proclaiming their real nature and activities? Ironically, this is precisely what many people do desire: 'really to know' something or someone, the

hope that at last reality and appearance will coincide. Clamence's previous discussion of the *enseigne* in terms of slavery,
and his ironic treatment, have already contaminated the idea
in the context of his discourse, so Clamence is able to conclude
that such a state of affairs would be hell.

To return to the paragraph on page 49, there is further
irony in the form it takes. It begins with Clamence's apparently
spontaneous invitation to look at the house, which is revealed
as a planned attempt to draw us deeper into complicity and
admit that there are things about ourselves we should prefer
to hide. Spider-like, Clamence weaves his web outwards, in-
voking a concrete detail in the street, appealing to his companion: 'n'est-ce pas?', recalling and drawing in the febrile
Parisian intellectual activity. Clamence's constant mental agitation is translated by the nerviness of the writing, the constant
flow of rhetorical devices: exclamation, interrogation, person-
ification, which is in constant tension with the tautness of the
paragraph's ironic structure. Clamence clearly takes pleasure
in his monologue, which prepares for the reader constant
surprise and the pleasure of recognizing Clamence's mind
at work.

The paragraph preceding, pages 48-49, shows Clamence
in different mood, such is the rapidity of his transformations.
It opens with a peaceful, elegiac passage appropriate to the
slow-moving canals and barges. Is Clamence 'really moved' or
is he adopting a lyrical pose? In place of our question, a
remark of the interlocutor's at this point brings an excitable
disclaimer: 'not a taste for morbidity, more forced admiration', which fulfils two functions: effectively puncturing what
might have been a weak moment with Clamence taken off
guard, and propelling Clamence onward — or upward — to
the theme of islands, which are what he 'really loves'. But just
as the reader might be about to pounce upon a 'real Clamence',
Clamence has turned round and punctured that balloon too:
'Il est plus facile d'y régner'; irony at his own expense which
becomes irony at the expense of the reader who might have
thought he had caught up with Clamence. Then, with the
abrupt transition to 'Délicieuse maison', Clamence, cordial as

ever, considers the subject closed. His elegant and affable
phrases move forward continually, smoothing over questions
and carrying the reader in his wake. The theme of islands
recurs later (152); Clamence's *hantises* lie in wait for him, he
who so carefully, and so competently, ensnares the reader.

Of course we distrust Clamence: he wants us to confess.
Paradoxically, however, our very distrust inspires a certain
faith in the nameless narrator, if not in J.-B. Clamence. For
the narrator knows very well what he is about: he is aware
of the traps and entanglements of language, dissatisfied with
self-satisfaction, the cut-and-dried response. The book is just
as much a 'mise en garde' as a conclusion. For the narrator,
the act of speech or writing, via J.-B. Clamence, is perhaps
the only solution to the problem of how to 'continuer, seulement continuer, voilà ce qui est surhumain' (120). There may
be no way of reconciling the many dualities of the human
condition, but perhaps if one sets them down, explores the
multifarious possibilities of reaction to experience, then maybe,
at some point, the direction and import, if not the detail,
might become clear.

Meanwhile, one has at least the richness, the exuberance
and vitality of language, the speech or writing itself: *morale
provisoire* which compensates in part for what, in the interim,
is being said.

9

La Chute: *Context*

'Après *L'Homme révolté*. Le refus agressif, obstiné du système. L'aphorisme désormais.'

Camus, *Carnets*, 1951

Between the publication of *L'Etranger* and the writing of *La Chute*, Camus had been concerned what he considered as a second stage in his work: 'le cycle de la révolte'. *La Peste*, which brought Camus an established reputation, presents the necessity for fighting against the plague and marks an important new direction: whereas Meursault had been a loner, Dr Rieux is an advocate of collective action. Revolt takes the form of action against injustice and evil. The book can be seen as an allegory of the German occupation of France and Resistance action, but Camus clearly intended it to have a more general import: man's hope lies in fighting to alleviate human suffering, even though this may be a Sisyphean labour. What is unsatisfactory in the book is the failure to account for human, moral evil: the symbol of the plague effectively removes evil from the ranks of men and situates it 'out there'. Nevertheless, the emphasis on the collective human condition and the pervading sense of compassion firmly established the humanist voice in which Camus spoke and contributed to define him as the moral mentor of a generation.

This impression was reinforced by the activities in which Camus engaged during the war and after. In the latter part of the war he was editor of the Resistance newspaper *Combat*, which with its clear reminder of essential principles and its refusal to compromise played a significant part in the atmosphere of liberation. Camus was convinced that the vacillation and collusion of pre-war politics had to be replaced by a sense of responsibility, democracy and a clear ethical direction. After leaving *Combat* he continued to be active both on questions of principle and on specific issues, in, for example, his repeated denunciations of Franquist Spain and his championing of Gary Davis's 'citizen of the world' movement. In part, then, *La Chute* is a satire on an image of himself which Camus sometimes unwillingly helped to project: a satire of humanist attitudes and the double presentation of Clamence as falling in his own estimation and as having a monopoly on truth. The fall of the image may be linked to a specific fall from favour: a bitter intellectual quarrel with Sartre.

After leaving *Combat* Camus continued to meditate on political and historical questions. As he had considered 'the Absurd' in quasi-philosophical terms in *Le Mythe de Sisyphe* as well as giving it fictional and dramatic form, so he felt the need to explore the notion of revolt in an essay, *L'Homme révolté*. The primary problem now is not suicide, but murder: what is there to stop one taking someone's life? Camus observes that men have an instinctive movement of self-defence against oppression, which he defines as revolt: a way of saying 'Thus far and no further'. Revolt, however, goes beyond self-defence, for Camus suggests that the spectacle of the oppression of others can provoke a similar movement of revolt in us. From this Camus concludes that this response of revolt is a characteristic of human beings in general: 'Je me révolte, donc nous sommes'. Revolt discovers the universal bond between human beings and the specific insertion of the individual into the human collectivity. So revolt provides a criterion for condemning murder in both general and particular terms.

But if this is so, why have men not yet established a peaceful and just society? Camus goes on to explore how revolt has been expressed in individual terms (la révolte métaphysique) and on the collective level (la révolte historique). In the first case revolt has tended to become total negation, as de Sade exemplifies, or it has turned into total acquiescence, as Nietzsche's progress shows. Both tendencies lead to nihilism, and both destroy the tension inherent in true revolt.

Camus observes a parallel movement on a wider scale: either collective movements of revolt, like the French Revolution, fall into negation, which provokes constant murder and terror or, like post-Marxian Marxism, they make a divinity of the 'necessary movement of history' and acquiesce in any means which may be employed in following the inevitable progression. The only example of true revolt Camus finds to cite is the 'meurtriers délicats', Russian terrorists of 1905, who were prepared to sacrifice a life for a life as a way of redeeming an assassination. Turning to art, Camus argues that the creation of a work of art is an act of revolt: the attempt to create form out of flux is paralleled by a refusal of what is: 'le monde romanesque n'est que la correction de ce monde-ci, suivant le désir profond de l'homme' (*P2*, 666). The final section of the book, entitled 'La pensée de Midi', is an attempt to extend the true revolt embodied by art into a historical perspective. Camus's contention is that the idea of *mesure* which he identifies with Mediterranean and particularly Greek philosophy, actualizes revolt and provides the criterion which will safeguard man against nihilism and totalitarianism: 'C'est la révolte qui est la mesure, qui l'ordonne, la défend et la recrée à travers l'histoire et ses désordres. L'origine même de cette valeur nous garantit qu'elle ne peut être que déchirée. La mesure, née de la révolte, ne peut se vivre que par la révolte' (*P2*, 704).

As with *Le Mythe de Sisyphe,* it is harsh to make simplification and summary criticism of a lengthy and complex work, but Camus's conclusion is unsatisfactory in a number of ways. The Mediterranean races appear as the new chosen people, safely delivered from the fog of German obscurantism. Camus tells us little about *mesure* except by tautologies, and the omission appears like evasion, particularly when one wishes to ask how *mesure* might be inserted into the historical dimension, and is confronted with a statement such as: 'Nous choisirons Ithaque, la terre fidèle, la pensée audacieuse et frugale, l'action lucide, la générosité de l'homme qui sait. Dans la lumière, le monde reste notre premier et notre dernier amour' (*P2*, 708).

Similar criticisms were raised by Francis Jeanson, when asked by Sartre to write a review of *L'Homme révolté* for *Les Temps Modernes,* a review founded and edited by Sartre. The principal argument of Jeanson's article 'Albert Camus ou l'âme révoltée', [23] is that Camus's premisses are unsound, that one simply cannot talk about revolution without discussing its economic and historical causes. Jeanson described Camus's approach as an attempt to situate revolution on the level of a 'pur dialogue des idées', which Jeanson considers tantamount to doing away with history. Although Camus was forced to recognize the place of history through the Resistance and Occupation, he was nevertheless reducing history to a type of second-degree evil, inferior in status to the primal evil of God's having condemned man to death and to the torture of 'the Absurd', but an evil still, from which Camus tries — or will try — to abstain. But if one denounces *démesure* only in its revolutionary form, does not this lead one to acquiesce in the equally violent *démesure* of capitalism? And, Jeanson concludes, how does this face of capitalism appear to the miner, to the Malagasy tortured by the police, or the Vietnamese 'cleaned up' with napalm?

Camus, obviously hurt by what he considered to be a misunderstanding of his book, replied in a 'Lettre au Directeur des *Temps Modernes*'. [24] He considered that Jeanson, in accusing him of neglecting the role of economics and history, had failed to appreciate that Camus had deliberately restricted his terms to a study of 'l'aspect idéologique' of revolt and revolution; that he had done so in no way denied the significance of aspects he had chosen not to consider. Not only had Jeanson misinterpreted, he had contradicted specific points Camus had made on the dangers of antihistoricism: 'mon livre ne nie pas l'histoire... mais critique seulement l'attitude qui vise à faire de l'histoire un absolu'. From defence, Camus passed to attack: the article seemed intellectually dishonest, operating on a double standard; accepting Marxism

[23] *Les Temps Modernes,* 8 (1952), 2070-90.
[24] Quoted in *P2,* 754-74.

as an implicit dogma and criterion, yet refusing to come out openly and defend it. Where Camus attacked specific injustices prevailing under Soviet communism, why did not Jeanson defend the Soviet labour camps? Further, how could one reconcile existentialism with its emphasis on human freedom, with a Marxist position which leads to a divinisation of history? Why is revolt possible in all other spheres, but not against the Communist party and state?

Camus's letter provoked a reply from Sartre, 'Lettre à Albert Camus', [25] arguing that Camus's practice of opposing one intellectual argument against another, in abstract and absolute terms, leads ultimately to quietism because it confers an inferior status upon action which, by its nature, is necessarily limited. One cannot abstract oneself from historicity and speak in absolute terms, and Camus is, regrettably, estranged from reality and its dynamism: preoccupied with man's struggle against Nature, he has failed to account for man's enmity to man.

Such, in brief, were the intellectual arguments; they were overlaid and intensified by a personal and vituperative tone for which Camus and Sartre were perhaps equally responsible. Since we are dealing with Camus, we can appreciate his bewilderment and confusion at the turn the quarrel took, the more so in respect of his previous friendship with Sartre and the comprehension, if not agreement, he may have expected from the *Temps Modernes* quarter. Overall, Sartre's arguments were probably more powerful and more convincing, but one cannot but admire Camus's stubborn rejection of a means-end philosophy and continued preoccupation with values. As in the story of the little Frenchman at Buchenwald, the laughter does not impinge upon the principle upheld. *La Chute* may be interpreted at one level as a satire of the *Temps Modernes* approach. A mention in Camus's *Carnets* for November 1954 reads: 'Existentialisme: quand ils s'accusent, on peut être certain que c'est pour accabler les autres: des juges-péni-

---

[25] Reprinted in *Situations, IV* (Paris, Gallimard, 1964), 90-129.

tents', [26] and critics have noted how specific accusations levelled
at Camus during the quarrel have been incorporated into the
text of *La Chute*. Clamence judging from on high, his formal,
definitive and denigratory pronouncements which permit of no
appeal, his refusal to admit evidence other than that which is
conducive to his case, his dismissal of the dust mote in his
own eye and denunciation of the beam in the other's, all may
be read in this context as a satirical description of Camus's
interpretation of the attitude of the *Temps Modernes* group.

It is difficult to assess to what extent the *Temps Modernes*
quarrel contributed to a further sense of failure on two different levels which Camus experienced during the early fifties.
Clamence, condemned to repeat himself anew to each interlocutor, undoubtedly represents to a degree the sense of steril-
ity as an artist which Camus experienced during that decade
even up to his receiving the Nobel Prize in 1958. Sensitive
to the honour done him, he nevertheless felt that the Prize
signified the crowning of an achievement, while privately he
felt that his work was merely beginning. Since completing
L'Homme révolté he had produced only *L'Exil et le royaume*
and *La Chute;* considerable enough, but Camus clearly felt
the lack of some major statement. The short story 'Jonas, ou
l'artiste au travail', in *L'Exil et le royaume,* describes the frus-
tration of the artist overcome by professional demands in-
vading his privacy, and domestic worries contributing to ar-
tistic impotence. For Camus also experienced a sense of failure
on the personal level, the inability to cope with demands made
upon him. In this perspective one can appreciate Clamence's
need to salvage some certainty from the ruins of doubt; one
appreciates all the more Camus's ironic appraisal of Clamence's attempts to halt his fall.

In a sense, then, *La Chute* represents a nadir for the
author personally and professionally, a writing-out of a sense of
specific failure and pervading guilt. At the same time one can
see in it signs of a rebirth, a new direction which, the more
unfortunately, is scarcely apparent in Camus's hitherto pub-

---

[26] Quoted by A. Abbou (*5*, p. 104).

lished work. In support of this, one may adduce Camus's sense
of relief that the 'cycle de la révolte' had been completed
with the writing of *L'Homme révolté*. [27] What direction might
his work have taken? Here one is reduced to more or less
founded speculation, but I think it is certain that Camus felt
that he had said all that he *had* to say, insofar as the times
we live in demand that one involve oneself and take up a
position. That position may have appeared unsatisfactory to
the *Temps Modernes,* but at least it had been stated. Henceforward Camus seems to have felt that he could allow himself
a more personal approach. It appears that the novel he was
working on at the time of his death, *Le Premier Homme,* was
an enquiry into his own past and that of his father, in Algeria.

In what direction does *La Chute* point? In one sense it
represents a purification, the exorcism of a need to conclude
which is clearly suspect. In another sense it is a statement
of ambiguity: the refusal to define, the obdurate offering to
the reader of something which is 'à prendre ou à laisser'. The
reader may conclude as he wishes: Camus has fulfilled his
contract simply by presenting. Thirdly, the novel presents,
in the thesis of Clamence, a certain 'exile' which is not independent, but dependent on the notion of a ' kingdom'.
Originally Camus conceived *La Chute* as one of the stories
composing the collection *L'Exil et le royaume;* the subject
demanded further development and the *récit* appeared separately. The stories of *L'Exil et le royaume* have in common
the presentation of the double theme, with the emphasis sometimes on the one, sometimes on the other, or on the equilibrium between the two. 'Jonas, ou l'artiste au travail' shows the
artist caught between the exile of conforming to public expectations or the kingdom of free, independent creation; in 'La
Femme adultère' the protagonist, Janine, experiences a mystical
communion with the night sky, a transitory experience since
she returns to the bed of her husband; 'Le Renégat' portrays
a man who, from an exalted, suspect desire to experience exile,

---

[27] 'Après *L'Homme révolté,* la création en liberté'. *Carnets* janvier
1942-mars 1951, p. 324.

conforms to the kingdom of evil. Taken together, the stories neither attempt to define precisely what is meant by the kingdom or the exile, nor do they conclude: the exile may not be irremediable, but one may not be able to live in the kingdom. It is illustrative to consider part of Camus's 'Prière d'insérer' which introduces the volume:

> *La Chute,* avant de devenir un long récit, faisait partie de *L'Exil et le Royaume.* Ce recueil comprend six nouvelles: *la Femme adultère, le Renégat, les Muets, l'Hôte, Jonas* et *la Pierre qui pousse.* Un seul thème, pourtant, celui de l'exil, y est traité de six façons différentes, depuis le monologue intérieur jusqu'au récit réaliste. . . .
>
> Quant au royaume dont il est question aussi, dans le titre, il coïncide avec une certaine vie libre et nue que nous avons à retrouver, pour renaître enfin. L'exil, à sa manière, nous en montre les chemins, à la seule condition que nous sachions y refuser en même temps la servitude et la possession. (*Pl, 2039*)

In this perspective, *La Chute* is perhaps closest to the story of 'le Renégat'. Clamence is a prophet in exile; the vision of the kingdom is dimmed, and he acts as though exile were the only reality. But, as I suggested, the preaching of the exile may, perhaps, give a glimpse of the kingdom.

Conclusion

ONE can scarcely read *L'Etranger* and *La Chute* without being forcibly struck by similarities between them. Chief among these, perhaps, are two common themes. Both works state the theme of duplicity: in *L'Etranger* in terms of the dichotomy between spontaneity and reflection, living in the body and living in the mind, in *La Chute* in terms of the duality inherent in the notion of falling. Secondly, but as a complement, the theme of guilt and innocence pervades both works, and the resolution of this antinomy reflects means of accommodating to duality. Meursault interiorizes certain of the processes associated with guilt yet retains a semblance of innocence by dying at the point at which instinctive living and rational living, closeness to experience and detachment from experience, innocence and guilt, are held in a fragile equilibrium. Clamence, more aware of the extent of culpability, makes a thesis of duality which allows him to conclude on one side: that of guilt. It is, henceforward, up to the reader to reintroduce the dual vision, correcting the *optique* suggested by Clamence. Both works, then, deal with ways of perceiving and relating to experience, both bring one back to individual choice, responsibility and continued struggle, in a world where nothing is given. Both present, fundamentally, a moral vision.

In this sense, both works have the status of 'myths of our time', even *La Chute,* that most resolutely anti-mythical of works. A myth might be seen as a statement, in the most simple and reduced of terms, of a fundamental problem of human existence, a statement which at the same time appears larger than life because it concentrates exclusively on that problem and shows its complete outworking, often literally to the death. Both works partake of myth in presenting a protagonist with whom it is virtually impossible to identify on the particular, psychological level, but who focusses attention on the problem of coming to terms with general human experience; who evades statements of the type 'Meursault is A', 'Clamence is B', to accentuate 'Meursault does X', 'Clamence does Y'. For this reason their significance can be extended: *étranger* applies to any aspect of experience with which one was not previously familiar; 'the fall' may extend to any conjunction of thought or experience which introduces duality. So in a very real sense one comes back to the dominant image, creator and justifier of the myth. This is perhaps the most profound link between the two works, the proof of common lineage.

However justifiable it may be to speak of communality of theme and of the place of works in the continuum of an author's *œuvre,* this should not lead one to evade an issue which is, after all, the *raison d'être* of a literary critic, and faced with which one tends to wriggle and protest like a devil in holy water. On what grounds does one decide, intuit or pontificate that one prefers one work to another? If one has dealt with two separate works one must, in the last analysis, come down and declare one's judgement, if only to submit it to the freedom of the reader.

I have, I hope, sufficiently expressed admiration for the two works separately to be permitted a comparison. *L'Etranger,* in spite of its comic elements, presents a certain high seriousness of tone which is absent from *La Chute*. This, I feel, links in with the pervading impression that Meursault is consistently referring to something which he does not make explicit, but which is positioned behind or beyond the book. So as readers we feel that if we could discover this key, we should understand Meursault. Although, as I have tried to show, *L'Etranger* is continually consistent within itself, it remains the case that a reading of *Le Mythe de Sisyphe* illuminates the novel in a way that a simple reading of the text does not. This doubtless contributes to *L'Etranger*'s remaining such a provoking and ambiguous work; certainly if this were Camus's only work of fiction, it would still secure for him a place as novelist in the annals of French literature.

La Chute, in addition to having the strengths of *L'Etranger:* the centrality of its theme to human experience, the ability to provoke and disturb, the tautness of structure whereby the different elements of the narrative are justified by the demands of the narrative itself, is all *there* in the text. While knowledge of the Camus-Sartre quarrel and of Camus's previous work obviously deepens our understanding of the 'whys' of the book, the *récit* stands firm on its own, focussing attention on the 'how'. Because it is so whole, it can afford to be more relaxed; at the same time as its movement is urgent and demanding, it introduces the subtler refinements of wit and dark humour, childlike glee and adult detachment; it offers the reader the constant surprise of feeling himself trapped and yet free, the delight of a style which alternates between classical severity and a yearning lyricism, which is aware of all the effects it can obtain and of the fascination of language itself, yet which can constantly undercut its own achievements. These are some of the elements which lead this critic at least to see in *La Chute* Camus's major work of fiction.

Chronological Table

1913   November 7. Camus born at Mondovi, Algeria.

1937   *L'Envers et l'endroit.*

1938   *Noces.*

1940   Camus moves to Paris to work on *Paris-Soir*. From this point onwards his permanent home is in France.

1942   *L'Etranger.*
Le Mythe de Sisyphe.

1943-1944   *Lettres à un ami allemand.*

1944   *Le Malentendu.*

1945   *Caligula.*

1947   *La Peste.*

1948   *L'Etat de siège.*

1949   *Les Justes.*

1950   *Actuelles I.*

1951   *L'Homme révolté.*

1952   Quarrel with Sartre in *Les Temps Modernes.*

1953   *Actuelles II.*

1954   *L'Eté.*

1956   *La Chute.*
Adaptation of *Requiem for a Nun.*

1957   *L'Exil et le royaume.*

1958   *Actuelles III.*

1959   Adaptation of *The Possessed.*

1960   January 4. Camus killed in a car accident.

Select Bibliography

A. EDITIONS OF CAMUS'S WORK

L'Etranger, Collection Folio (Paris, Gallimard, 1957).
La Chute, Collection Folio (Paris, Gallimard, 1956).
Théâtre, récits, nouvelles, edited by Roger Quilliot, Bibliothèque de la Pléiade (Paris, Gallimard, 1962).
Essais, edited by Roger Quilliot, Bibliothèque de la Pléiade (Paris, Gallimard, 1965).
Carnets mai 1935-février 1942 (Paris, Gallimard, 1962).
Carnets janvier 1942-mars 1951 (Paris, Gallimard, 1964).
Cahiers Albert Camus 1. La Mort heureuse, edited by Jean Sarocchi (Paris, Gallimard, 1971).
Cahiers Albert Camus 2. Paul Viallaneix 'Le premier Camus' suivi de Ecrits de jeunesse d'Albert Camus (Paris, Gallimard, 1973).
Cahiers Albert Camus 3. Fragments d'un combat, edited by Jacqueline Lévi-Valensi and André Abbou, 2 vols. (Paris, Gallimard, 1978).
Journaux de voyage, edited by Roger Quilliot (Paris, Gallimard, 1978).

B. GENERAL AND CRITICAL STUDIES

1 Lottman, Herbert R., *Albert Camus: a biography* (London, Weidenfeld and Nicolson, 1979).
2 Cruickshank, John, *Albert Camus and the Literature of Revolt* (London, Oxford University Press, 1959), reprinted Greenwood Press, Westport, Connecticut, 1978.
3 Fitch, Brian T., ed., *Albert Camus 1 (1968): autour de 'L'Etranger',* La Revue des Lettres Modernes, nos. 170-174 (Paris, Lettres Modernes, 1968).
4 Fitch, Brian T., ed., *Albert Camus 2 (1969): langue et langage,* La Revue des Lettres Modernes, nos. 212-216 (Paris, Lettres Modernes, 1969).
5 Fitch, Brian T., ed., *Albert Camus 3 (1970): sur 'La Chute',* La Revue des Lettres Modernes, nos. 238-244 (Paris, Lettres Modernes, 1970).
6 Fitch, Brian T., ed., *Albert Camus 4 (1971): sources et influences,* La Revue des Lettres Modernes, nos. 264-270 (Paris, Lettres Modernes, 1971).

7 Quilliot, Roger, *La Mer et les prisons: essai sur Albert Camus,* revised ed. (Paris, Gallimard, 1970).

CRITICAL STUDIES OF 'L'ETRANGER'

8 Banks, G. V., *Camus: 'L'Etranger'* Studies in French Literature, 30 (London, Edward Arnold, 1976).
9 Barrier, M.-G., *L'Art du récit dans 'L'Etranger' de Camus* (Paris, Nizet, 1962).
10 Bersani, Leo, 'The Stranger's Secrets', *Novel,* 3 (Spring 1970), 212-24.
11 Brée, Germaine and Carlos Lynes, Introduction to *L'Etranger,* Methuen's Twentieth-Century French Texts (London, Methuen, 1958).
12 Champigny, Robert, *Sur un héros païen* (Paris, Gallimard, 1959).
13 Fitch, Brian T., *Narrateur et narration dans 'L'Etranger' d'Albert Camus: analyse d'un fait littéraire* 2nd revised ed., Archives des lettres modernes, no. 34 (Paris, Lettres Modernes, 1968).
14 Fitch, Brian T., *'L'Etranger' d'Albert Camus: un texte, ses lecteurs, leurs lectures: étude méthodologique,* Collection 'L', 2 (Paris, Larousse, 1972).
15 Frohock, W. M., 'Camus: Image, Influence and Sensibility', *Yale French Studies,* 2 (Fall-Winter 1949), 91-99.
16 Pingaud, Bernard, *'L'Etranger' de Camus,* Collection 'Poche critique', 1 (Paris, Hachette, 1972).
17 Rey, Pierre-Louis, *Camus: 'L'Etranger': analyse critique,* Collection 'Profil d'une œuvre', 13 (Paris, Hatier, 1970).
18 Sartre, Jean-Paul, 'Explication de *L'Etranger',* in *Situations, I* (Paris, Gallimard, 1947).

CRITICAL STUDIES OF 'LA CHUTE'

19 Barchilon, Jose, 'A Study of Camus' mythopoeic tale *The Fall* with some comments about the origin of esthetic feelings', *Journal of the American Psychoanalytical Association,* 19 (April 1971), 193-240.
20 King, Adèle, 'Structure and Meaning in *La Chute',* *PMLA,* 77 (1962), 660-67.
21 Ngoc-Mai, Phan Thi, Pierre Nguyen Van-Huy, avec la collaboration de Jean-René Peltier, *'La Chute' de Camus ou le dernier testament* (Neuchâtel, La Baconnière, 1974).
22 Nøjgaard, Morten, 'Temps et espace dans *La Chute* de Camus. L'importance des faits linguistiques comme signaux physiques de la structure littéraire' *Orbis Litterarum,* 26 (1971), 291-320.
23 Rey, Pierre-Louis, *Camus: 'La Chute': analyse critique,* Collection 'Profil d'une œuvre', 1 (Paris, Hatier, 1970).